D0276585

Letting Go

Letting Go

Dilemmas for parents
whose son or daughter
has a mental handicap

Ann Richardson
Jane Ritchie

Open University Press
Milton Keynes · Philadelphia

Open University Press
12 Cofferidge Close
Stony Stratford
Milton Keynes MK11 1BY
and
242 Cherry Street, Philadelphia, PA 19106, USA
First published 1989

British Library Cataloguing in Publication Data
Richardson, Ann
  Letting go: dilemmas for parents whose
  son or daughter has a mental handicap.
  1. Great Britain. Mentally handicapped
  persons. Care
  I. Title   II. Ritchie, Jane
  362.3'8'0941

  ISBN 0-335-15841-2
  ISBN 0-335-15840-4 Pbk

Library of Congress Cataloging-in-Publication Data

Richardson, Ann.
  Letting go.

  Bibliography: p.
  Includes index.
    1. Mentally handicapped—Great Britain—Family
relationships. 2. Parents of handicapped children—
Great Britain. I. Ritchie, Jane Beaglehole.
II. Title.
HV3008.G7R53   1989   649'.8   88–25483
ISBN 0-335-15841-2
ISBN 0-335-15840-4 (pbk.)

Typeset by Gilbert Composing Services
Printed in Great Britain by J.W. Arrowsmith Limited, Bristol

Contents

Preface

This is a book about parents with adult sons and daughters living with them. The parents are of very different ages and live in very different circumstances, yet they share one situation in common: their son or daughter has a mental handicap. In this book, we explore their feelings about having their son or daughter living at home as well as how they view the idea that he or she might move away. We look at parents' efforts to prepare themselves and their son or daughter for long-term separation and consider the experience of a few parents whose son or daughter has recently left home. The whole book is about the very difficult problem of 'letting go'.

This book is not only *about* parents; it is also, by careful use of discussions, seen *through the eyes of* parents. Having explored parents' views and experiences, we have tried to set these out in their own words. We have not aimed to create an academic study and have not set our findings in the context of other writings. Instead, we have tried to create a vehicle for understanding parents' points of view, collating and organizing what they have to say. A few comments on what people outside the family can do to help, as well as on how parents themselves might respond to the issues raised, are provided in the concluding section.

We have prepared this book with several different audiences in mind. First, we hope it will prove helpful to parents themselves. It will not, we suspect, tell them so much that is new, but it may help them to see that many others are struggling with the same issues. We also hope it will prove helpful to anyone who is concerned to increase their understanding of what it is like to have a mentally handicapped son or daughter at home. This may be a professional working in the area of mental handicap, whether a social worker, a medical professional, a teacher or the like. It may also be people with no particular professional reason for such interest but a concern to extend the boundaries of their own knowledge*.

Two interweaving themes will be found throughout the chapters of this book. On the one hand, there is the very distinct nature of the situation faced by parents whose son or daughter has a mental handicap. There are few families who do not experience special burdens and restrictions, and few who do not at some point question their own ability to cope. In addition, these parents tend to feel a strong sense of responsibility to their son or daughter, arising in part from the particular vulnerability of a handicapped child. Furthermore, the long-term outlook for their son or daughter, in terms of where he or she will live and who will provide support and friendship, sooner or later becomes a cause for concern. These and other such special circumstances deeply affect parents' perspective about a move from home.

On the other hand, there is much that is the same between these parents and all parents with sons and daughters at home. First and foremost, there is the enormous bond of parental love which dominates and colours all the decisions they are forced to take. Like all parents whose children pass out of adolescence into adulthood, these parents have to take stock of their position and may need to find new ways of relating to them. They have a very similar task of teaching their son or daughter to become independent and preparing him or her for a life elsewhere. As all parents, they need to come to terms with separation, facing the prospect that the family may not always be together. Finally, like many other parents, they tend to suffer deep anxieties about whether they have struck the right balance, whether they have done 'right' by their son or daughter. The problems will be heightened by the existence of a handicap, the decisions will be more difficult, but the underlying issues are very much the same.

A short note on terminology needs to be added here. At present,

---

*A shorter book, devoted to the policy implications, has also been prepared. See Ann Richardson and Jane Ritchie, *Making the Break: parents' perspectives on adults with a mental handicap leaving the parental home.* London, King's Fund, 1986.

the term 'people with learning difficulties' is preferred to the more traditional language used in this book. We have continued with the term 'mental handicap' because it tends to be the term used by parents.

This book arises from a study, carried out over two years, about mentally handicapped adults and the move from the parental home. This was undertaken in two local authority areas and involved discussions with over one hundred parents, some in groups and some individually in their own homes. All of these parents had handicapped sons and daughters living with them. In addition, a small study of parents whose son or daughter was already living elsewhere was carried out in another area. To provide some context for this research, a postal survey of all parents with mentally handicapped adult sons and daughters living at home in the two areas was carried out.

It may be useful here to give a brief picture of the people who 'speak' throughout this book. They include parents whose sons and daughters have all kinds and levels of mental handicap. Some are extremely handicapped, both mentally and physically, unable to do anything for themselves, perhaps without speech. Others have only a very mild mental handicap and are able to go out alone, carry out ordinary household and personal tasks and be reasonably self-sufficient. They range in age from their late teens to middle age. The parents range from their forties to their eighties. They come from a range of social backgrounds, some living on quite low incomes. Most of the sons and daughters go to local training centres during the day, but a few stay at home or have local jobs. All names have been changed here to preserve anonymity.

It will be important to remember that this book focuses on parents who have handicapped *adults* at home. It does not consider the views of those parents who find alternative care for their children when they are first born or still of school age. The book is also concerned only with the views of parents; it does not consider the move from home from the handicapped person's point of view. In both cases, these would have been different pieces of research, with quite separate perspectives.

It is essential here to give due recognition and thanks to those who contributed to this book. First, to the Joseph Rowntree Memorial Trust which provided the necessary financial support. Second, to our co-researchers, Jill Keegan and Kit Ward, who carried out the interviews with enormous sensitivity and skill.

Third, to the three members of a small advisory group, Oliver Russell, David Towell and Jan Porterfield, who gave us consistently sound advice. Finally – and most important of all – to the parents who agreed to take part in the research. We asked them to explore their innermost thoughts, doubts and anxieties on one of the most difficult questions any parent has to face. We hope we have done justice to the depth and honesty with which they responded.

CHAPTER 1

Four Families

If you have a child, you have to let go, don't you? It's very tough if you can't. It's a measure of your love if you let them go, but it isn't easy, believe you me. It isn't. It's very difficult.
Mother of Martin, aged 24 (left home a year earlier)

Introducing the issues

For any parent, thinking about a son or daughter leaving home raises a host of complex emotions. It is the end of the long period of their child's dependency and the beginning of a new relationship between them. It is likely to be a time of re-assessment, especially for those mothers whose principal role has been the parental one. For some, it may be met with a sense of relief, that attention can finally be turned to new issues. For others, it may represent primarily a sense of loss. In either case, it is a period of considerable change within a household. It brings to a head the changing interests of parents and their children and their differing needs for one another. While many families experience the transition with relative ease, for many others it can prove a very difficult time.

These considerations tend to be heightened in the case of a son or daughter with a mental handicap. The whole question of independence is more difficult, because of the greater risks involved and the consequent protectiveness of parents towards their handicapped children. In those families where the son or daughter has been at home over many years, relationships within the family may be particularly close. The idea of a move from home is rarely raised by the son or daughter, so it is the parent who must take the initiative. There are also very difficult questions about where the son or daughter might go.

There are two key periods when the issue of a move from home tends to seem most pressing. First, there is the time when the son or daughter is moving from adolescence into young adulthood, symbolized often by leaving school. This is the time when many non-handicapped children would be looking towards a move from home, either to get work, to go to college or to set up their own marital home. Many parents want to give their adult sons and daughters the chance to lead a life as close as possible to that of non-handicapped young people. Recognizing the importance of providing them with an opportunity to live away from home, such parents begin to take a hard look at the options that are available to them.

At the other end of the spectrum, many parents, having cared for their sons and daughters well into adulthood, find themselves no longer able to cope. This may be because of age, illness or being left as a single parent through widowhood. Their offspring may have lived in the parental home all their lives and have only very limited experience of separation. Such parents can become very concerned about what will happen to their son or daughter, especially if they might have to face a move which is abrupt and unplanned. They therefore seek help to ease the transition before a moment of crisis.

The issues arising in the case of young and older families are clearly very different. It is not simply that parents' perspectives differ according to their own age. It is also that the experience of a move has very different implications for parent and 'child' alike. For a young person with a mental handicap, a move away may seem a natural progression to a new life; for an older one, it is likely to be viewed as the loss of what had come to be seen as a permanent home. For the parents, too, the move is likely to mean very different things. For younger parents, it may be seen as the source of a new freedom, the opportunity to do what they want like other people of a similar age. For older parents, in contrast, it may seem to be 'the beginning of the end', with little to devote themselves to for the remainder of their lives.

Four families

In order to illustrate the range of dispositions parents can have towards this move, four families are described below. In certain key respects, these families have many characteristics in common. All four handicapped children have just reached adulthood. The parents, too, are about the same age, in their mid-forties to mid-fifties. More significantly, all of the young people have fairly severe handicaps, although these differ somewhat in their particular manifestations. All have had some experience of short-term care away from home, and one has recently moved away permanently.

Given these many similarities, it is striking that the parents hold very different views about seeing their son or daughter leave home.

Sara

Sara is 19, sensitive, affectionate and very beautiful. She lives with her parents, both in their fifties, and with her 21-year-old sister. Two other sisters are married and live near by. The family lives in a comfortable house on the outskirts of a Northern town, and have a very close relationship.

Sara has a very severe mental handicap due, it is thought, to brain damage at birth. She has no speech, is doubly incontinent and has periods of hyperactivity. She is also slightly 'spastic down one side'. During the day, she goes to the special care unit at the local Adult Training Centre.

Sara needs a great deal of care and attention: 'She can't do anything for herself. You've got to feed her; she can't grip things; I think she'd starve if we didn't feed her. We've tried to teach her to eat, especially when she was younger, but there's nothing there at all; she doesn't seem to learn anything, even by repetition, she doesn't respond at all.' Being doubly incontinent, Sara 'makes an awful lot of washing'. She also tends to wake continuously during the night, getting only a few hours sleep.

Getting around is a particular problem: 'She walks on her toes; you've got to help her. In a confined place, where she knows her surroundings, she's not so bad, she'll get across from one side of the room to another, but if you went outside in a strange place, she'd trip over something. . . . You can't take Sara shopping; you've got to grip her arm, because she's off, just wanders off or starts jumping up and down making a noise.' Communication is difficult: 'She's slightly autistic; she won't look at you with her eyes. She says, "mama, mama"; she used to say odd words when she was younger. . . . She goes through phases.'

Both Sara's parents are quite certain that she should stay with them at home. Her mother, who does most of the work of looking after her, has no doubts: 'I shall look after Sara [as long as] I can. That's my philosophy, because I think she's our responsibility. I know a lot don't; they just bung them away as quick as they can, but I think you've brought them into the world, they're your responsibility as long as you can cope.' This is not simply a matter of duty: 'I know people would think you're crackers, but you do love them. I mean, you love them an awful lot. I love her an awful lot. They're special, aren't they?'

Her father, equally devoted to his daughter, says how much he enjoys having Sara at home: 'We love Sara, you know. She's lovely. When she was away, this house weren't the same. You get used to her, even though she's not doing a lot. Now, if I switch on that television, you can bet your life that she'd get up and go stand in front of it and I'd have to get up to put her back down again; this goes on all night. We talk to her and shout to her in fun . . . so when she's not there you miss her. . . . I suppose it's like you'd love a dumb animal, it's something like that, although she's not dumb. . . . I can't explain it. Because she's Sara, I suppose, she's ours. . . . So we're going to look after her while ever we can.'

Sara has spent short periods of time in the local hospital for mentally handicapped people and in local hostels, both for children and adults. Because she has just turned 19, she can no longer go to the children's hostel where her parents felt she was well looked after. They are not particularly happy about the choices now available: '[The hospital] didn't look to have much staff to cope with them and that put us off straightaway so we never let her go back again. . . . She had bruises when she came home. Well, she is liable to fall into things and anybody a little bit better could do something to her, a kick or something like that.'

This experience has affected Sara's parents' views about letting her go for short stays: 'You see, you've all this worrying you, when you let them go somewhere. You want somebody you can trust, that you think will look after them. . . . It's a lot easier having her here and looking after her and worrying about her than having her away somewhere and worrying about her, isn't it? It's not easy, but it's easier. Put it that way.'

Sara's parents have a clear picture of the type of residential place they would like to see available: 'The same type of thing for living as they have in [special care units] – specially trained staff, friendly and not too officious. Somewhere smaller, not too many . . . Somewhere where you can trust people to look after her, to care for her. Somewhere with security.' At present, the only place which they feel meets these criteria is their home.

When they think about the long-term future, Sara's parents have no notion of where she will go: 'We never think about Sara moving on, do we? We can't; we know it will never happen. It'll be us that will move on first, so what's going to happen to her then? It worries you a bit wondering what will happen to her. There's nothing wrong with Sara physically; she could live a long time.' Certainly, they do not want her sisters to have to take on her care: 'I don't expect [them] to look after her. I never have. They all know that, as far as I know.'

This issue is a real worry: 'I think there should be more guarantees to people like us who've looked after their children – let's face it, there's some that's looked after them an awful lot longer than we have and they've still got them at home – that there will be somewhere for them. Nobody seems to be able to guarantee you anywhere.' For now, and the foreseeable future, Sara will stay at home: 'As long as we can cope . . . she's going to stop here while ever we're here or either one of us'.

But Sara's older sister is concerned: 'My Mum and Dad are getting to a certain age where obviously it's not going to be much longer before they can't deal with Sara, purely through age . . . If they can come up with somewhere that's nice for her to go, that me Mum and me Dad can be taken and shown and they can sort of let her go for a day at a time, a night at a time, and work on it that way so that me Mum and Dad get used to her being away and Sara gets used to her surroundings . . . that would be kind on both parts. Obviously it's going to happen one day, when Mum and Dad are gone, it's going to be us, you know, that are going to see her wherever she is. And I'd hate to see her in one of those hospital type places – it would break my heart.' But despite her concern that her parents should be preparing themselves to let go, she – like them – can see no suitable alternative.

Malcolm

Malcolm is 19 and the youngest of three. His two older sisters are married but live nearby, while he continues to live with his parents at home. Malcolm's parents are in their late forties and his father is a bus driver.

Malcolm was born with brain damage and also has a physical handicap. He is not able to do much for himself because he lacks coordination. His mother finds his behaviour very wearing: 'He can say a few words, but can't make a sentence. . . . He also screams a lot.' But Malcolm is a kind person, loves his family dearly and lives very happily at home.

Malcolm has been away frequently for short periods, largely to give his parents a break. He has been to the local hospital several times, which were 'quite happy experiences' and to the local hostel, which did not work so well. His parents do not know what happened but he came home both ill and listless: 'He'd never been like that before. He wanted to come home; he didn't want to be left again.' His parents therefore decided not to 'let him go again. It's as simple as that.'

Malcolm's parents feel a real dilemma about what to do about his future. On the one hand, they want to keep him at home and 'care for him'. On the other, they wonder if this is really the best thing for him: 'We know that he does get lonely and we wonder if he would be better off with his own kind of people.' But they do not believe that a hostel would look after him properly – clean his teeth, wash him, and so forth: 'The thing is, he's all right for a fortnight, but is he going to be happy if they don't toilet him properly and he gets sores and everything? Is he going to be happy then?' Whatever the number of staff, his mother does not believe that 'they can look after him like what I and my husband look after him'.

Malcolm's mother admits that she is 'torn two ways'. She loves her son deeply and wants to protect him: 'he's just like my baby'. Above all else, she wants him to be well looked after. She is therefore willing to keep him at home and care for him. But she is also concerned: 'What if something happened to us – somewhere would have to be found.' Moreover, there is the worry that if something happened to one, the surviving parent might be extremely isolated and lonely, with only a handicapped son for company. Yet both have promised that they would not let him go away.

If Malcolm did leave home, his parents would like him to go somewhere with a lot of staff 'so that he'd have a better chance of being properly looked after'. They would also like him to be with people less – not more – handicapped than himself, since 'he copies people and he would learn from those with more highly developed skills'. It is not that they feel places do not exist; they have seen television programmes about places that were 'really good, first class', but being private, they were expensive. 'If we could get somewhere like that, we'd gladly let him go', but there were real doubts about their ability to afford it.

But there is also an additional dilemma. Whatever any place was like, they would find it very difficult to let Malcolm go. They question whether anywhere can be a real substitute for home: 'Home gives him his own things.... He likes all his own bits and pieces and paraphernalia – home offers that – the other places don't'. They also feel that Malcolm is not very strong: 'You know, when you nursed a baby that's ill all the time and and so frail, and he is frail, it makes you protective towards him. If he were more robust I don't think I'd be as worried.' Finally, there are feelings of guilt; having brought him into the world, his mother feels she caused his condition and therefore owes it to him to provide the best care she possibly can.

The upshot of these many considerations is inaction. Although the future needs of their son are constantly in their minds, they try to avoid thinking about it too much: 'You don't dwell on it a lot because it's such a big decision. Because your life kind of revolves round him ... If he went away permanently, you know, I think it would take at least six months before we ever felt anything in life was normal.'

Simon

Simon is the 20-year-old son of parents in their mid-forties, who have two other teenaged sons at home. His father works in a car factory and his mother also works part-time. Simon's handicap, which is fairly severe, is thought to derive from brain damage at birth, although it was not confirmed until he was two. He goes to an Adult Training Centre during the day.

In his parents' words, Simon is a very soft-natured and sociable person: 'He's very easy to get on with; he never gets into tempers or anything. He's very amiable and a very lovable person. Everybody does love him. We've never kept him in; he's quite safe here, we're on a cul-de-sac and he'll go out there for half an hour and he doesn't go away.'

Simon is also quite capable in many ways: 'He speaks; we understand him, but some people have a problem, but on the whole he speaks quite reasonably ... He doesn't really write, he hasn't got any idea of money, but he's got a good memory ... He washes himself after a fashion, can't do his shoelaces or buttons. He gets dressed, everything seems to go on inside out, back to front, shoes on the wrong feet, but apart from that I think he's basically like a five or six-year-old.'

It was always the parents' view that they should keep Simon at home until he was 16 and finished school. Then, they felt, they should be thinking of him moving on: 'I don't want to do it any more than Simon wants to do it, but we just feel it is something that has got to happen. Particularly as he is the oldest and we've got other boys. They've always been very good and looked after him, but they're both going to do their own thing now. We never wanted him to go away [when he was younger]; he was no problem. Even now, really, he's not a problem except we get a bit frightened of us getting older and there being no one to look after him.'

Simon's parents are very concerned about the long term future: 'I would never expect the other boys to look after him, or relations, because I just don't think that's on. I think it's better for him as well to be away. There's so many people I know at the Centre who have never been away from their parents, some of them are 35 or 40. Well, I think it's terribly cruel. Their parents aren't always going to be there to look after them ... You must make provision before they're too old to adjust. I think this is really why I've persevered with it, because I feel it would be easy to turn around and say, "oh, well, forget it all". I know that isn't the answer.'

Parting is not seen to be easy, however: 'I don't think either of us will ever be ready. Not ever, unless something drastic happened in the family, then it would be entirely different. But then it would be an awkward time to send Simon away, so I think if he's got to go away, he's got to go when things are normal and all running smoothly. I think to have to cope with more than one thing, like losing me, that would be absolutely terrible for him to have to go away from home at the same time.'

The issue is again the source of some agony: 'I accept it, because

I feel I've got no choice. This is the way I look at it. I feel I haven't got a choice and the sooner it's done, the better, and I just hope that Simon accepts it all right. But, of course, the thing is not irrevocable. If it was totally and utterly wrong, then he would have to come home again. But I think it would have to be very very wrong for me to reverse the decision. . . . I think it's right for everybody else – not for Simon. The other boys, and my husband and myself; the whole family against one.'

Simon's parents have discussed the idea of leaving home with him, pointing out that most people leave home as they get older: 'I try to get through to him, basically, that he's getting older now and people don't stay with their parents all the time. My nephew left home to join the police force; he doesn't live with his mum. I don't live with my mum. I try to put it to him that way, adults don't always live at home. I mean, when he gets cross with me, he always tells me he's going to go off and get married . . . But that is the only way I can talk to him about it; of course, we'll still come and see him and he'll still come to see us, like we do nanny and grandad. I think he accepts this reasonably well. It's always in the future.'

In anticipation of his eventually moving from home, Simon's parents have used short-term care since he was eight years old. He has gone for one or two weeks, three to four times a year, first to a children's hostel and now to an adult one. He has never adjusted to going away: 'He's accepting this one a bit more now that he's got a bit more adult, but you know he's so close to me, he tends to follow me around a lot . . . He says, did I book it? Why can't I cancel it? and he counts the days. He wants to know exactly when I'm going to fetch him and what time I'm going . . . He's just not happy and he keeps on about it.'

Simon is now going to the hostel once a month, each time for a week, in preparation for a move away. The hostel is gradually stepping up the time he spends away, because there is a chance of a permanent place in a few months. Simon's mother thinks that the longer the periods become, the easier it will be for him: 'I think Simon's biggest traumatic thing is leaving me every time and I think perhaps he'll be happier in himself once he's there for longer periods and he hasn't got that effort of leaving me every time.' The eventual plan is that Simon should live in the hostel permanently but come home for breaks. And although none of them will ever be ready for that permanent break, his mother is quite certain that, for Simon, it will be in his long term interest. He will, after all, be 21 and at an age when the whole family should be thinking of him 'moving on'.

Danny

Danny is 24 and was brought up alone by his mother who was widowed shortly after Danny's birth. His mother is in her late forties and now works full time as a play group organizer. Two years ago, he moved to the local hostel.

Danny was brain damaged at birth and has a severe mental handicap; he is also epileptic. Although he can do some things for himself, like washing, he needs some help with dressing and other daily activities. He also can't go out alone because 'he has no idea of road safety'. Danny loves snooker and also music: 'He can manage his own record player and although he can't read, he can distinguish one record from another, even when the labels are the same'.

As a single parent, Danny's mother had always been concerned that she should see Danny settled before anything happened to her. Danny therefore spent several periods of short-term care in a nearby hospital, 'trying to build him up for long-term care'. On later occasions, Danny had come home with bruises, looking strained and unhappy. This led his mother to think 'no more'. But it also deepened her worry about where Danny would go when she could no longer look after him.

The balance was tipped to 'let go' when the opportunity arose for Danny to go to live in a new local hostel. Although it was the 'most terribly difficult decision', Danny's mother felt strongly that it was in her son's interest: 'I had to look at his long-term future. You do owe it to them. Unless the parent looks at it, it just doesn't happen. I think you need to know in your lifetime that he's going to have the right placement.'

In the months that followed the decision, Danny's mother tried to reconcile herself to the impending separation. It was, as she says, 'an awful period, really. You change your mind a hundred times. I knew it was going to be a completely different lifestyle, because you get in a routine, really. You are constantly sitting here waiting for coaches and you are governed by the clock, really, for what you are able to do. I knew all that was going to alter. In many ways I didn't really want to look at it at that time. I think you've got so many mixed emotions that it's terribly difficult to sort anything out at all.'

Preparing for the move was particularly difficult: 'I didn't know how to start preparing. I mean, how does one suddenly alter their complete lifestyle?' She did take Danny for tea at the hostel, however, to meet the staff and to see his new home. She explained to him that that was where he would be going to live. But she was never sure how much he really understood. She also found it difficult to prepare herself. It was 'difficult to think rationally' about it. Deep down, she felt that 'no one would ever care for Danny like I have. And you want to feel that they can't do without you.'

There were other feelings as well: 'I think you feel guilty that you are throwing them into the outside world. It's letting go, really. I don't think anyone really wants to let go of their children. And it's also frightening that, yes, they can live without you as well. You don't think they possibly could and then suddenly you realize that, yes, they can. You are not the be-all and end-all.'

The day of the move was terrible: 'There's so many mixed emotions that you're going through and they're all guilt emotions. You're guilty that you're putting them into care – that you're not keeping them home when you've still got the health and strength to look after them. You feel like you're betraying them, that he's got a right to be at home, why am I doing this to him? It is really like going through a bereavement.'

She got through the first difficult weeks by keeping herself very busy. She found a part-time job and visited friends, trying to give herself no time to dwell on Danny's absence. Otherwise, she said, she might have been tempted to bring him home again. The weekends were particularly difficult, when the house was empty, and she missed him enormously.

But Danny settled down well and now his mother feels he has a better life than she 'could ever have hoped for'. He goes out more than he did – to the pub, to church and to clubs – and does things which his mother never 'dared let him'. He has made some good friends at the hostel and has an active social life. Every month, Danny visits his mother for the weekend, but returns quite happily to what is now his home. She feels Danny has now adapted totally to the separation: 'I think Danny has let go of me – he's sort of severed the string.'

Although Danny's mother has some reservations about the

hostel – both the size (24 residents) and the fact that the staff cannot give as much personal attention as she feels her son needs – she is nonetheless certain that the decision to move him there was right. She has adapted to her own way of life, enjoying the freedom to suit herself more and to go away when she wants to. She sees Danny frequently; visiting is encouraged by the hostel and he comes home regularly. Above all, she is comforted by the knowledge that if anything should happen to her, Danny will be all right.

Four very different situations have been set out here. Sara's parents consider her to be their responsibility and, seeing no suitable alternative, expect her to remain at home over the long term. Malcolm's parents are beginning to think about the possible need for a move. Simon's parents have established a clear plan for a move and are preparing their son for his transition from home. Finally, Danny's mother has made the break, putting her son in a local hostel, and is content that he is happy there.

Yet all these families share – or shared – a common difficulty in beginning to think about letting go. The idea that their son or daughter will leave home is probably the hardest decision they will ever have to make. This is partly because of considerations affecting their son or daughter and partly because of considerations affecting themselves. The feelings of love and protectiveness, the desire to continue the parental role as long as possible, and the concern for what life will be like elsewhere affect most families.

There are, of course, many other kinds of situations which could be portrayed. Some parents, particularly those of severely handicapped sons and daughters, are desperate to find a suitable place outside their home. Others, in contrast, see little problem, having agreed that their son or daughter will move to the care of another family member in due course. The nature of the family, the nature of the handicap, the nature of their relationship with one another all differ to some extent from one home to another. Yet there are a large number of common questions. It is to these that the remainder of this book is devoted.

CHAPTER 2

Caring at Home

What does home give anyone?... Home is home, isn't it?
Home to me seems the proper place to be.
                                    −Mother of Richard, aged 39

All parents with handicapped sons and daughters living with them
face difficult questions about both the long-term and the more
immediate future. They need to think about what will happen
when they can no longer cope or when they die. At the same time,
they must also consider whether they should look after their child
until they can no longer cope or, instead, seek other provision
before that time. But parents' responses to these questions cannot
be understood in isolation. They have already made a whole range
of decisions to get to this point. Their views must be seen to arise
out of a context in which their circumstances, attitudes and
assumptions all play a major part. There are, not surprisingly,
substantial variations between families in all these respects.

Sons and daughters at home

People with a mental handicap cannot be described as if they were
all the same. Their individual behaviour, dispositions and needs
differ as they do among the rest of the population. Although they
have a 'special need' in common, this too can vary greatly
depending on the nature of their handicap, any associated physical
or behavioural problems and the range of abilities they have been
able to develop. Looking after a son or daughter with a mild

handicap is very different from looking after one whose handicap is very severe. Caring for someone with serious physical disabilities presents additional special problems. There is consequently a range of differing experiences and attitudes among parents with a handicapped son or daughter at home.

The continuing presence of a handicapped son or daughter in the household brings out two highly complex sets of emotional responses among parents. On the one hand, there is a very positive side, arising from a strong parental bond and the pleasure in having a loved child at home. On the other, there is a negative side, arising from the stress placed on a family by a handicapped member. The relative strengths of these two conflicting aspects of home care depend in large part on the nature of the son's or daughter's handicap. They are also affected, however, by the amount of support available to parents or, alternatively, the degree to which they feel a sense of isolation. Most commonly, both love and stress are present to some degree.

The positive side

On the positive side, there is no doubt that most parents with handicapped sons and daughters at home feel a great love for them. While their lives may revolve heavily around looking after their child, the everyday tasks of this care come to be seen as wholly natural. They are undertaken as part and parcel of the parental role. Indeed, as with any family, the looking after and the loving are frequently bound up together. This is well described by the mother of Beatrice, mildly handicapped and in her late twenties:

> In the morning I go in with a cup of coffee and she'll say 'my mummy' and she'll put her arms around me. And I always have a cuddle session every morning. Oh, yes, I nearly get strangled; that's why I've got quite a long neck. And I have a cup of coffee and she'll get out of bed. And we do the same routine, the same timing, the same thing every morning. Get her breakfast, see her off or wait for the coach together. I go out with her, see her in the coach. I stand by waiting at half past four and watch her come out. And her little face beams all over. Yes, you see? The same routine every day.

The sense of fun, the playing together that goes on within any family whose members enjoy each other's company, is also present here. This may be a physical rough and tumble, the tickling that ends in hugs and laughter. It is also just doing things together, like taking walks or doing work around the house. This involves fathers as well as mothers: 'Julie became my shadow. She convinced herself that there were lots of things I couldn't do without her. If I was doing woodwork, she was there to hand me the screws.'

But this sense of fun together can also be of a more mental kind. It may be gentle teasing or the sharing within families of the well-understood joke. Robert's mother, for instance, whose 30-year-old son has a mild handicap, explains:

> We have our own type of conversation, you know. I don't call him Robert, I call him Trebor – that's Robert backwards. He'd say to us 'What day is it today?' I don't say it's 'Wednesday', I say it's "Nesthurday". I take the end bit of Wednesday and the beginning part of Thursday... All that sort of thing. We have a lot of jokes and that's what he likes. He's got a good sense of humour.

This has gone on, of course, for a long time. In ordinary families, the fun between parents and children often does not survive the development of adolescence, although it may return later. Here, in contrast, it can grow and blossom over many years, creating an ever stronger bond between parents and their son or daughter. There is no natural break, no point at which it seems 'normal' to see it come to an end. Indeed, life with the handicapped son or daughter seems utterly normal to these parents.

There is something else that happens to many parents who keep their son or daughter at home in their later years: they feel *young*. For most parents, the time when their children have grown up and moved out of the household is a period when they must face their own slide into later life. The span of years with children in the home is often found to be surprisingly short. For parents with handicapped sons and daughters, in contrast, there may be no such break. Furthermore, whatever their age, mentally handicapped people often seem to have the lifestyle and tastes of teenagers – records and pop music and the like. The presence of these 'young people' in the house can dramatically affect the self-image of their parents: 'You don't feel as though you're growing old, because you've got to do the things that they want to do', and 'they keep you on your toes.'

Parents who continue to have their handicapped sons and daughters living with them often express the love they feel for them. They say they have 'that little bit extra' for their handicapped son or daughter and that he or she, in turn, 'gives us more love than all the others'. As one mother puts it:

> He needs me and every day it's a sort of compliment with someone. It makes you feel good. There is someone who loves you and it's a lovely form of love. There's no ifs and buts about it. It's a pure love and it's lovely.

Indeed, parents stress their view that their child is not essentially a handicapped person but a loved human being: 'It's the love and affection for you. I've got a handicapped son, he's 52. I wouldn't change him for half a dozen graduates.'

The darker side

But there is another side of the coin, the inevitable stresses and strains. These can be considerable and there are few families for whom they are wholly non-existent. Furthermore, they are felt to affect all members of the household. Other children living at home, for instance, are commonly expected to do more than a normal share of helping with a sibling. More significantly, the amount of parental attention such brothers and sisters can have is often very limited; family outings and holidays may be heavily restricted in number or scope. Many brothers and sisters are said to feel inhibited about inviting their friends to their home and go to considerable lengths to avoid doing so. Parents are often quite concerned about these questions.

The greatest stresses, however, are felt by the parents themselves, especially the mothers who generally carry the burden of day-to-day care. There is often, of course, a lot of extra work brought on by the presence of a handicapped person in the household: extra cleaning, washing and so forth. This can be particularly a problem where the handicap is very severe; some handicapped people are doubly incontinent, for instance, and unable to feed or wash themselves at all. There may also be other sorts of demands, again particularly where the handicap is more severe. One father describes this graphically:

> For the first 16 to 17 years, we never slept at night. We never

slept totally through the night. You were always up and down to him, two, three, sometimes six times a night. And all he wanted was to turn on his side again. So you were physically tired.

Where a son or daughter is at home all day, it can also be difficult to carry out the normal tasks of running a house. The mother is unlikely to be able to take a quick trip to the shops, while the strain of trying to shop with her son or daughter can be very great. Where there are also frequent epileptic fits, the need to be 'constantly on the alert' can be especially difficult:

> [The fits] have always been the biggest problem, because you literally can't take your eyes off him. I mean, the times I've just caught it. He'll just keel right over. The only time he is safe really is when he is sitting down. So, going to the toilet, bathing, you always have to be there. I can't get on and do something, just like that. If I want to hang some washing on the line, he has to sit down and he doesn't want to sit down.... Sometimes I give up.

Parents also find there are problems just keeping their son or daughter amused and happy:

> We're getting older. You haven't got the energy, you haven't got the fresh ideas. You get tired, terribly tired. And, of course, he's getting older so things that amused him at one time don't any more. He'd sit and do a puzzle, he's fed up with that, so he'll find something else. And he gets fed up with that.

Lives become restricted in all kinds of ways, some not necessarily very obvious to those not close to the family: 'I'm afraid we haven't been to church for years and years, because, well, he sings so much out of tune that everybody used to turn around and look'.

Effects on parents' lives

The sense of never having time on one's own clearly affects large numbers of parents. It is very difficult for mothers to work, or have any other day activity, outside the home. It can also be difficult to find time for themselves within the home; many parents say 'your life is never your own'. Again, this is most difficult where the handicap is most severe; as one mother explains: 'He follows me around, he's always with me. Wherever I go, he's behind me. . . . He's there all the time. After a while, that gets on top of you.' This can also affect parents' time together, or their time with friends:

> He always wants to be there . . . in the middle of things. He's not rude or belligerent. But you couldn't ask friends around and have a quiet evening, because he would dominate the conversation. So you just don't do it.

At the extreme, some parents find themselves with the sense of being almost permanently 'stuck' at home. Here is the mother of a very severely handicapped daughter of nineteen:

> She didn't want to go out; in the summer holidays, she'd be in for days, days on end in the garden. Just sitting there or playing with some water. And I used to think if only we went out for a picnic or went to the seaside or went shopping . . . it wouldn't be so boring. Because she didn't want to go, she made it really difficult when we were out. She wouldn't walk, or she'd start scratching you or spitting at people. In the end, we just thought if she doesn't want to come out with us, we won't force her.

These accumulated stresses sometimes affect parents' health, both physical and mental. Parents seem impressively resilient and reluctant to feel sorry for themselves, but it is not uncommon for things to become too much for them:

> Now that Tom's grown up, he's no trouble, but when he was younger, many times I used to go and shut myself in the toilet, cry and cry and cry and think, you know, 'God, why is it me?' But there's thousands of other parents that do that. He had a temper, dreadful temper and he used to stamp his feet and scream.

There is also, for some couples, a considerable increase in marital strain. The demands of a handicapped son or daughter at home, coupled with the inability ever to get away by themselves, can take a toll. As one father explains: 'It forces this terrific wedge, sort of emotional wedge, with the continual 24 hours a day, seven days a week caring. That has a terrific cumulative build-up on you.' The handicap seems to bring out on a larger scale marital problems suffered by many couples when they become parents, the divergent needs of mothers and fathers giving rise to new tensions. One mother explains one aspect of the problem:

> My husband hasn't a lot of patience, he likes a quiet life. Most of the time, I suppose, I cushioned him from the children. . . . I found that I coped fairly well until he retired. But for the first year, it was dreadful, because I found I just wasn't coping with Jim, I was coping with my husband's reaction to Jim.

Parents caring for adult sons and daughters have a relationship to them in many ways more akin to those of parents with young children. This is true both for the positive side, the close bond between parent and child, and the negative, the heavy demands and restrictions imposed. If anything, parent–child relations in this context seem to become more – rather than less – close. At a time when most parents would be turning their attention to other interests, the activities of the parents with a handicapped son or daughter are still closely bound within the family. The result is an adult son or daughter who is 'one of us', a family that is a trio instead of a couple. Doing things together, going places together, becomes the norm, a 'way of life'.

Of course, these families have been living with their situation for some time. They have had many years in which to come to terms with their restricted circumstances and accept their son or daughter's limitations. They have organized their lives around their handicapped son or daughter, so that the restrictions he or she imposes are largely taken for granted. Those for whom the burden was too great or who chose a different care arrangement for their sons and daughters when they were children are not among their number. It may be, too, that handicapped adults are less stressful than handicapped children; many parents speak of the much greater burdens experienced when their sons and daughters were younger.

Perhaps surprisingly, parents' feelings of being burdened do not seem to increase with their own age. One might expect parents to cope quite adequately while in their fifties and early sixties, but to find their situation increasingly difficult as they themselves become elderly. This does not appear to be so. The parents who seem under the greatest stress are those whose handicapped sons and daughters are most difficult to cope with, whether violent, subject to frequent fits or simply uncommunicative and constantly depressed. Parents whose own health is a source of concern are naturally somewhat anxious, but they do not generally attribute a higher degree of strain to their son's or daughter's presence in the household. Even very elderly parents do not seem unduly burdened by their situation. Whatever concern they express is directed to their son's or daughter's long-term needs, not their own immediate welfare.

Help and support to parents

To what extent are parents' dispositions to keep their sons or daughters at home affected by whether they receive the amount of help they feel they need? In order to answer this question, some attention must be given to both sides of the 'equation'. Some parents feel little need for assistance of any kind, while others are desperate for any help they can get. Some of the difference here lies in the degree of severity of their son's or daughter's handicap. But some parents have the good fortune to have a wide range of helpful friends, relations, and local professional people, while others seem largely isolated.

Family and friends

It is widely accepted that in most families the main responsibility for care falls on the mother. She is the person who provides most of the physical care, offers much of the emotional support and does a lot of the worrying. This is partly because she is traditionally the one who is at home, whereas the husband is out at work. It is also because of a common acceptance of a division of responsibilities within a marriage. The role of women as the mainstay of the household, common wherever there is a person needing care, is probably nowhere more evident than in the families described here.

What forms of help are available? Undoubtedly the most important source of support to most mothers comes from their husbands. This includes not only emotional support but also all sorts of practical assistance. In some families, for example, fathers play a key role in the physical care of their son or daughter. In others, husbands provide little or no help at all: 'I've never had a husband I could talk to. He's never helped. When she needed so

much care, there were only *one* to give it and that were me.'
Clearly, mothers whose husbands are actively involved with their
son or daughter have a distinct advantage over those who are left
to cope on their own. They also seem to approach the whole
question of a move from home with less sense of stress.

There are many additional sources of both practical help and
emotional support to parents. First, there is the help provided by
their other children, whether still living at home or in their own
homes nearby. A number of parents are able to ask these sons or
daughters to sit in, gaining themselves either the occasional
evening off or a more extended break. Some have help from other
family members, although the absence of any help from this source
is indicated quite frequently:

> My husband's people have never really wanted to know.
> They don't visit now. I go to see my mother-in-law, but she
> was no help in the early days. My sister lives nearby, but she
> doesn't really have a clue about anything.... I've never
> bothered people.

Some parents also gain considerable help from neighbours, for
instance, in keeping a friendly eye on their son or daughter in the
area. One mother describes her son's life:

> I find that living in a village, they accept him. He goes down
> to the pub and he plays darts. He can't take the scores or
> anything but he enjoys a game of darts. He's got a pushbike
> and cycles all the way to the local town to see his friend....
> He's always out.

The presence of such help and understanding is greeted with
considerable gratitude; its absence is conversely the cause of some
bitterness. Many parents are quite distressed by the lack of public
sympathy for or understanding of mentally handicapped people.

Professional help

Another important source of help to parents lies in social workers
and other professionals with whom parents come into contact.
Here, parents' stories are less happy. Although some receive a
great deal of assistance from a variety of professional sources,
there is a high degree of disappointment with the amount of
attention received. This is especially visible with respect to social

workers; indeed, many parents are uncertain whether they 'have' one at all. In the words of one mother, who had never seen a social worker until her son was 16: 'We didn't know what a social worker was. I thought a social worker was for somebody who'd been in trouble or something. They've just never bothered. Never.' Parents are often concerned that their social workers keep changing, so there is no continuity. Yet they very much want a lifeline to some official help: 'I think they should come and give him a call every year or so. Just so you can sit and talk.'

A few parents have been very distressed by what they felt to be callousness from a social worker at one time or another. Although these are only a minority, their stories serve as an important reminder of the ways in which outsiders can affect parents in this situation. One example gives the flavour of the problem. In inquiring about short-term care, a couple had raised the question of longer-term residential care with a social worker:

> She said, 'Oh, now, if anything happens to you, we'll find a bed for her somewhere.' Well, it makes me feel I don't want to see any social workers again. If that's how they were – throw my child in and give her a bed somewhere – I don't want their help.

There are some parents, of course, who are resistant to what they see as interference from outside. This may be because there is no felt need for help or because of a lack of understanding. Again, social workers come in for considerable complaint: 'Usually what they do is come and give sympathy and you give them tea. Which isn't a great deal of help.' One father puts it this way: 'If you have social workers in, it's to help with their training. . . . We help *them*.' Some parents suggest that social workers need to be more sensitive to what they want; one father, rejecting a suggestion that he look into alternative care for his daughter, notes: 'It's probably in their books in black and white "parents need a rest", so every parent's got to be asked.'

On the other hand, some parents do find their social workers to be helpful – finding short-term respite care, for instance, or giving advice about cash benefits. This seems to work best where they have established a good relationship over time, knowing how a family thinks on key issues. Parents are only too ready to praise where a social worker has visited the family on a regular basis over the years. They particularly appreciate those who give time to their handicapped son or daughter as well as themselves.

A number of other people can also prove helpful to parents. Their general practitioner is someone from whom they can get assistance if needed and in whom parents sometimes feel they can place their trust. The manager or other staff at their son's or daughter's day centre are also used by quite a few parents for advice or help. Indeed, they are often the only professional group with special knowledge of mental handicap with whom parents have any regular contact. Voluntary organizations, such as Mencap, can also play a useful part in parents' lives. While many belong, however, few describe themselves as very active; these groups tend to be used more as a source of social activities for the son or daughter than as one of support for themselves. Yet parents like to know that they are there.

The amount of help received does not appear to be a major influence on the decision to care for a handicapped son or daughter at home. Having a helpful family and friendly neighbours clearly makes it easier to cope and access to someone official provides added confidence that help can be acquired as necessary. But supported parents are no more certain than isolated parents that they want their son or daughter at home. Indeed, mothers who receive substantial support from their spouse seem to approach the whole question of home or alternative care with less sense of stress. They are therefore *more* – rather than less – willing to think about a move from home. In particular, they are more able to consider the question from their son's or daughter's point of view.

The decision to keep a son or daughter at home

Except where a child is diagnosed as having a mental handicap at birth, there is generally no one moment when the decision to keep him or her at home is an urgent one. Instead, it is a continuing question which tends to sit in the back of parents' minds, forming a backcloth to a host of other decisions. For some, it is a very real issue over a considerable period of time; for others, it begins to be pressing only when their own health or age forces it on them; for still others, it is not a live issue at all, having been resolved many years before in the parents' own minds.

There are, in essence, two separate decisions here. The principal focus of this book is the decision to begin to look – or not to look – for alternative care. But this is necessarily preceded by an earlier decision: to keep a son or daughter at home over the years. Some attention must be given to this first decision here. For many parents, the very question of why they took this particular course sounds odd; it seems overwhelmingly the most natural course to have taken. Their children, now adult, are at home because they have always been there. Indeed, there may never have been any 'decision' at all; the idea of seeing them move away may never have arisen. Yet there are a number of different underlying reasons for parents choosing to look after their son or daughter at home. It may be useful to try to disentangle them.

A parent's responsibility

Perhaps one of the most widely felt reasons for keeping a handicapped son or daughter at home is a sense of parental responsibility. This may begin at the time of birth or diagnosis, but it tends to remain right through adulthood. It is expressed in a number of different ways, all having a common theme of what a parent owes a child. One parent speaks for many: 'No one asks to come into the world; he belongs to us and it's up to us to look after him'; and another 'I just feel I owe it to him. . . . I'm his mother and I just owe it to him to look after him; that's all'. This view is strengthened in some cases by a determination on the part of parents to be self-reliant: 'He's nothing to do with anyone else; he's my cross to bear.' It also receives a great deal of approval over the years. Family, friends and neighbours are all likely to confirm how 'good' it is of the parents to carry on the daily job of looking after their handicapped child.

Parents' sense of responsibility is often given considerable reinforcement by key professionals at critical stages in their lives. Doctors and nurses can play a crucial role at the time of birth or diagnosis, when parents are highly vulnerable. This was even more clearly the case twenty or thirty years ago. A mother who raised the question of institutional care when her child was two, explains:

> We were told in no uncertain terms, he was our responsibility, he was our child and it was up to us to take him home and look after him. That's what we were told . . . which we did. So all the way along the line, there's never been any suggestion that he belongs anywhere than with us.

Two related messages are conveyed here: that parents must provide the necessary care and that they should not question this position. The second can prove of considerable significance over the long term. As parents may already be highly sensitive about their situation, the potential disapproval of someone in authority may be very harsh indeed. The issue may not be raised again for years.

Growing accustomed

But having taken an initial decision early on, many families care for their son or daughter at home simply because they have become accustomed to it and adapted themselves to their situation. Sometimes, this adaptation has developed slowly as the fullness of the handicap becomes more appreciated:

> It's so gradual. I didn't know Amy was handicapped, really. I knew there was something wrong with her, but I was always told she was a slow developer, you see. As time goes on, you realize it's something much deeper than that. You tend to accept it. Well, you have to accept it or else you'd be miserable all the time.

These parents' lives slowly become so organized around the handicapped son or daughter that they become wholly accustomed to the restrictions imposed; as one mother notes: 'It's grown on us. He's not a handicap to us.' They carry on reasonably happily and can see little reason to question the existing arrangement. Life with their handicapped son or daughter becomes a normal life and their routine a normal routine. Here is the mother of a 20-year-old daughter with a severe handicap:

> It is only when she's not here that I realize what a different day I have to other people. . . . To me, it's normal. It's normal that I cut up her food tonight, it's normal that I do all the things for her, it's normal that I get her ready for bed tonight, it's normal for me to take her to get her hair cut, to take her to the dentist, to take her everywhere. It's normal for me to do it, but when she's not here and I don't do it, I realize that I could have a life of my own and that other people don't live like that.

Love and companionship

There are a substantial number of parents, however, whose decision to keep their son or daughter at home stems from what can only be described as parental joy. These parents may also have adapted to their situation, but they have done so with enormous pleasure. They want their son or daughter to remain at home essentially because they have fun together, although not perhaps unalloyed with difficulties. The parents' view of their situation is essentially a contented one: 'He's a happy boy, he's always got a smile on his face.' Some parents express this even more strongly: 'My life is David. It has been for such a long time that I can't visualize it any other way. And I don't think I would want to.'

This picture tends to take on a new poignancy as parents age, one partner dies, and the other parent is left on his – or more commonly her – own. The son or daughter becomes a companion to the parent, a provider of help in the household but also someone to do things with. An elderly widowed mother talks about her daughter: 'A lot of people think that they are a burden on us. But Linda's not a burden on me, see. She's like a companion, more than a burden.' These parents find it particularly difficult to think about their son or daughter moving away.

Quite often, the relationship between parent and child seems to turn over time into reverse, so that the parent becomes emotionally dependent on the son or daughter, or on the situation of having him or her to care for. This appears to be particularly common among mothers, both those left on their own through widowhood or divorce and those forced to be the sole carer, although married, because of lack of paternal interest. This dependency is well-recognized by parents themselves; they readily speak, for instance, of being 'lost' or 'at sea' when he or she is away. Especially for older mothers, these parents tend to feel they have retained a close family involvement, unlike others of their generation. The position is well summed up by a mother with a son of nearly 40: 'I can't imagine life without him. . . . It would be all wrong. Life wouldn't be complete. There would be something missing. A big bit missing.'

The proper place to be

Most parents also feel, however, that for their son or daughter home is 'the proper place to be'. The family home provides a crucial sense of security, accepted as natural for small children yet unchanged in the case of handicapped adults. They have a very clear idea of what it is that home means to their son or daughter: 'Everything. Everything. Love, cleanliness, Godliness, the lot.' The greatest stress is put on the emotional side: 'Family, affection, love, understanding. Even when you get angry withi him, the anger is parental anger, not the anger of a stranger.' Home is a place where their sons and daughters can feel protected and loved, where there is automatic and natural acceptance of what they are and what they can and cannot do. The basic security of parental love is what it is all about. As one mother puts it simply, 'There's no substitute for your own love, is there?'

But there are other more practical aspects of home, which parents stress should not be overlooked. It is a place where their sons and daughters can have their own room and their own things around them. They can play their records or watch television when they like and generally have greater freedom to come and go as it suits them: 'He has no obligations, he can go in there, he can go upstairs, he can do what he wants – what he likes to do himself. He's free.' Such freedom, it is felt, would not be found elsewhere.

Finally, many parents feel that home is where their son or daughter *wants* to be. Many have had experience of residential care on a short-term basis, such as a week's stay in the local hostel. Parents feel they quite enjoy the occasional visit but would not wish to move there on a permanent basis. Some are said to find even a very short stay difficult:

He's a home boy. It's a terrible thing to have to say, but he wouldn't even dream of going anywhere without his mother. So even a week, or a weekend, that he goes to the hostel is in some ways a little bit of torture to him.

It is with these differing circumstances and attitudes that parents of handicapped sons and daughters find themselves caring at home. Some have a son or daughter who is easy to be with and some have a very heavy burden of day to day care. Some have a great deal of help and some have little at all. But they are all 'caring' both in the sense of looking after and in the sense of feeling deeply about their son or daughter. It is, after all, what being a parent is about.

CHAPTER 3

Perspectives on the Move from Home

> I'm caught between the devil and the deep blue sea. I want to
> see him settled before anything happens to me, but I don't
> want... to see him go away before that time.
>
> Father of Colin, aged 42

Parents' views on keeping their son or daughter at home arise from
a complex set of emotions about the nature of their role as parents
and the needs of their child. Their perspectives on the move from
home are essentially the same question in reverse. 'Should we be
caring at home?' becomes 'Should we be looking into other
provision?' For parents who have looked after their sons or
daughters into adulthood, this is not a simple decision. No parent
finds it easy to think about and some find it distressing to discuss.
Even those who have come to some decision often express
considerable doubt about whether it is right. Yet all parents know
that their son or daughter will have to move at some point, if only
after their own death. It is the urgency of the issue which varies
from one family to another.

There are in essence, two separate issues for decision. First,
whatever the age of their son or daughter, there is the question of
thinking about some form of alternative care soon or in the
foreseeable future. Second, there is the question of the long-
term – what parents expect to happen when they can no longer
cope. But in either case, there is a quiet separate matter of making
(and effecting) a particular plan. Not all parents have begun to
think about the move of their son or daughter from home, either
now or in the future. But even where they want to find a place,

many years may intervene before any move occurs. This may be either because no suitable provision can be found or because parents are not ready or willing to take that final step. This chapter explores parents' thinking about the move from home; the planning and effecting of a move is discussed in Chapter 6.

Parents' positions: an overview

In considering the move of their son or daughter from home, there are three possible positions parents may hold. First, they may be positively seeking a move. Some of these may feel that the time has almost come for a move, but are not in any sense of urgency about it. Others may be desperate, anxiously seeking some relief from the stresses of looking after their son or daughter. Many of these may have been looking for a suitable place for some time. Some parents plan the timing of a move from an early period, deciding that their own retirement of their son's or daughter's completion of school should serve as the impetus for change. Others may find the need for a move catching up with them unexpectedly, perhaps because of their own failing health. Whatever the reasoning, parents tend to know when the time has come. As one mother puts it:

> Everybody expects to be tied down with children. But when it goes on for 29 years, it gets a bit long. . . . There comes a stage where you want to see the children go off and give you a bit of peace and quiet.

Some parents, in contrast, have a very different perspective; they do not want their son or daughter *ever* to leave home. They feel that their son or daughter belongs at home and that it is their job to provide the necessary care. This is part of a wider concern to keep their family together. As a mother of a 30-year-old daughter declares: 'As long as I have any breath in my body, I want to hold my daughter with me. Right to the last. . . . I don't want to part with her. She's too much a part of me.' Some of these parents may expect their son or daughter to be cared for by a sibling when they die, but some have no real idea of where their son or daughter will go.

Finally, some parents are fundamentally ambivalent on this issue, in two minds about whether a move should take place and when. They know that a time will come when the move should be made, but they do not want to see it come. Often, they set a time limit, five or ten years say, after which they expect something will need to be done: 'I know deep down that he will have to go somewhere, I mean, he won't always be able to live here. It's always on my mind, always.' Some say they will take action 'when we can't cope' or 'before we can't cope' but acknowledge that it may prove difficult to recognize when that time has come. Some of these parents are still young, and see the issue as one for the future, but many retired parents essentially hold the same position. In the words of one mother: 'It's something you shelve.'

It is very difficult to know how many parents feel one way and how many another. The question is a difficult one to ask and the answers are by no means clear cut. Only a small minority of families with handicapped adults at home appear to be actively seeking alternative arrangements and very few indeed seem to have firm plans. Most families either seem quite certain that they do not want a move to take place or have conflicting emotions about the question. Perhaps surprisingly, there appears to be little difference here according to the severity of the son's or daughter's handicap.

Older parents might be expected to be more anxious to find a new home for their son or daughter than younger ones, but in fact any variation is in the opposite direction. It is older parents who feel most strongly that they want to keep their son or daughter at home and younger parents who are concerned to think through the process of making the break. This may be due simply to a generational difference in attitudes. Younger parents, it is often suggested, are less willing to tolerate the long-term conditions experienced by the older generation and thus have different views about the move from home. But it is not at all clear whether these views remain constant or change as parents themselves become older. Of course, looking only at those parents whose son or daughter is currently at home may give a biased picture; many parents will have made the decision at an earlier point.

The problem of making the break

Parents' views on the issue of a move are essentially the converse of their feelings about keeping a son or daughter at home. Parents tend to feel not only that they *ought* to care for their son or daughter at home but also that they *want* to do so. Most have come to adapt their lives to their situation and many derive enormous satisfaction from it. Many parents feel that no one else would ever care for their son or daughter as they do. They also commonly feel a very strong love for their son or daughter, which makes them want to hold him or her at home. In the words of one mother: 'It's rather a shock when you realize. You've had a handicapped child for years and you feel they've taken over your life. I think you suddenly come to realize you need that child. You need that person.'

A strong sort of tie

How, then, do parents approach the question of making a break? Some essentially decide to ignore the question of a move, to carry on until nature takes its inevitable course. These parents are often very clear about their position. It is well summed up by a mother, herself well over the age of retirement, talking about her son of 39:

> I would never ever want him away from me – I mean, there are some excellent places, don't get me wrong. It's just – while he's got a home and a family, I just feel that's where he should be. . . . I suppose it's a bond between you. There's a strong sort of tie that no matter how you try, you can't really untie it. It's there; and I just couldn't let go. I couldn't.

A number of parents acknowledge a very real worry that they are thinking too much of their own needs by choosing to keep their son or daughter at home. This is not only a matter of companionship but also one of growing parental dependency. Often, of course, the two aspects are heavily intertwined. One mother explains:

> I live on my own. She's the only companion I've got. Since my husband died, I feel like a ship without a rudder already. I just don't know what direction I'm going. And if she were to go now permanently, maybe she would be a lot better, but I think I should just sink.

Nor is this a view held solely by mothers. Here is one elderly father, discussing his reluctance to try short-term care for his son: 'It's selfish, because you're not giving them the opportunity to see if they can cope by themselves or without you. . . . We are being selfish. I am. I wouldn't part with my lad for all the tea in China.' Another father turns the question around, with his own question: 'Have you got children? Would you want to put yours in a hostel, to say "I'll see you in the next year, duck"? Now you answer me that!'

Nonetheless, it is often the mother who is most wrapped up in the caring role and who would feel most lost without it. Caring for her child is, after all, what defines the way her life has been spent. It begins with the small baby, continues with the handicapped child but does not cease as her son or daughter passes into adulthood. This loss of her central role is well summed up by one mother who compares her involvement with her handicapped daughter to that with her other daughters: 'They've got their own lives and they go off and you're not needed any more. You're more or less redundant. Whereas with a handicapped daughter, you're not. You're dependent on each other, more or less.'

'Putting them away'

But there is no question that parents are also thinking beyond their own needs when considering this issue. Many are responding to the commonly accepted view of what they feel any responsible parent would do. The idea of 'putting him away' is still very strong: 'I hear some people couldn't care less. Let them go in hospital and that's it. They don't bother with them anymore. But I couldn't do that.' Indeed, the expressions parents use to refer to the decision to seek alternative care are striking; none are positive and few are even neutral in tone. They talk of 'signing her away', 'having him committed', 'pushing him away', 'pushing her on', 'farming them away', 'sending him away' and, very simply, 'getting rid of him'. One mother suggests a son or daughter who leaves home is 'a sort of a castaway'. Another, noting that she could only be looking for another home for her son 'because I was rejecting him', adds: 'It would be to say, "he's a bother, a nuisance, let's get shot of him, let's put him in a home".'

There is also the simple problem that many parents find it difficult to think of their mentally handicapped son or daughter as adult. The chronological age may be 18 or 20 or even 45, but the mental age may be closer to that of a child. A number are additionally physically small. Parents call them 'boys' and 'girls', reinforcing the view that they are not really adult at all. As one father puts it: 'I think he is our child; he always will be our child. So, you don't really send a child away. Even at 30, he'll still be a child, even though he'll have a booming deep bass voice and have a beard, he's still a baby really.'

It's their future

But some parents consider that there is a positive side to seeking an alternative home for their son or daughter. Indeed, some express this as a rather different aspect of the issue of parental responsibility: the duty to develop their sons and daughters to their fullest capacities. At its broadest, this involves preparing them for a move out of the parental home in the same way as non-handicapped sons and daughters. They want their sons and daughters to be able to leave home when they reach adulthood and start new lives elsewhere. As one father states: 'You have to come to terms with yourself, because it's not my life, it's Christine's. It's not my future, it's *hers*. I don't pretend it's easy, but it has to happen.'

Experience of other care

One major influence on parents' feelings about making the break is their experience of alternative provision. Many families with handicapped sons and daughters have had some experience of residential care on a short-term basis and a few on a long-term basis as well. The overall impact of this experience on parents' willingness to see their son or daughter leave home needs to be considered here.

Parents' feelings about their own indispensibility as carers for their children are clearly affected by their opinion of the care provided elsewhere. If this is good, they may become confident that others, too, will love and protect their son or daughter. If it is bad, however, they will easily lose any sense of trust and revert to a reliance on their own resources. The strength of parental response to a bad experience by their son or daughter outside the home can endure, literally, for years. It can prove one of the most significant influences on their attitude to the move from home.

There are considerable numbers of parents whose only attempt to place their son or daughter in residential care was at a time when the sole provider of such care was the local mental handicap hospital. A few parents speak well of the care provided, but many, perhaps not surprisingly, do not. One mother of a son in his late thirties, for instance, had placed him in a hospital for a short period when he was a child:

> When I came back I was horrified. I was shocked beyond compare. He was on an adult ward – a 9-year-old boy. And the things that a brain-damaged person told him were disgusting. Now he couldn't make it up because he doesn't know how to lie.... I was horrified. And [I decided] never again. He's never been out of my charge since.

The loss of trust may be particularly severe where parents' criticisms appear to go unheard or their deep concern unrecognized. One mother, for instance, who was bitterly unhappy about the hostel used for a short stay on her social worker's strong urging, noted:

> Apparently there wasn't enough supervision and I said this to the social worker and she said, 'Well, do you know', she said, 'this is a very strange thing you should say that about the house. Because I reverse my car in their driveway, but I've never been inside to see what it's like.'

Parents, after such an admission, can be unwilling to try again for a long time.

Although such experiences reinforce parents' sense that no one can look after their son or daughter as they do, good experiences can, of course, have the opposite effect. Many parents are often pleasantly surprised at how well their son or daughter is treated in a short stay at a local hostel: 'He loved it, you know. It was a holiday for him as well as us.... He thoroughly enjoyed it.' As they build up a sense of trust in other providers, they come to see that it is not necessary that they shoulder the burden of care on their own. They also see the gains in independence, perhaps accompanied by a sense of achievement, made by their son or daughter. This all serves to reduce the feeling that the responsibility to look after him or her has to be unending.

Ambivalence on this question is often very close to the surface. It is expressed in one of two directions. Some parents are concerned to demonstrate their willingness to make the break if their son or daughter wanted it. As one mother puts it: 'If she liked and she wanted to go, I mean, I wouldn't stop her. It would break my heart for her going, but I wouldn't stop her.' On the other hand are the parents who find it difficult to admit that it might be a good thing for their son or daughter to move on. One father speaks frankly to his wife on this matter: 'You'd miss him, but it would be a big relief off you, wouldn't it. Tell the truth. You're not condemning him because you say you could manage without him, you know. Everybody knows that sometime in their life a son or daughter is going to leave.'

Leaving the nest

Some parents have strong feelings about the place of all of their children, whatever their age, within the home. There are a number of parents who have no wish to see *any* son or daughter leave home. Although they know that their adult offspring will want to get married or move out for other reasons, they see their departure as a real loss for their household. One mother of five says:

> I felt that they were rejecting me. You know, wanting to get married and go away from home. I felt the loss of each and every one of them as they went. . . . It took a long long time to get over the fact that one of my flock had flown.

These are the more traditional families, perhaps quite large, who feel they belong together. Often, their married sons and daughters live nearby.

Some parents feel that there is no real problem here. They suggest that too much can be made of the need to see a son or daughter settled. They have watched their son or daughter cope with a range of changes and adjustments, such as the death of a loved grandparent or even parent, without great fuss. They naturally assume that he or she will adapt when necessary: 'When it happens, she'll make do and mend.' For many parents, of course, there is no great urgency about the move.

The reluctance to see sons and daughters leave home is commonly reinforced by the lack of any initiative from them. Unlike non-handicapped post-adolescent children, who often choose to leave home as soon as they are able to do so, people with a mental handicap are not usually in a position to make any move.

They typically know neither the alternatives nor their own potential to sample them. They thus put little or no pressure on parents for a different arrangement. Furthermore, there is no equivalent pressure from other parents to see the situation as abnormal, for instance compared with other mothers with adult sons at home. Indeed, as has been shown, the pressure appears to be in the reverse direction, with parents feeling potential disapproval if they 'put away' their handicapped child.

Some parents are, however, concerned about their son's or daughter's happiness about being at home. Some sense a longing for greater independence:

> These youngsters, they're no different to normal young-sters. . . . They come to an age where they want to be independent and they're not able to express their feelings or look after themselves. That's where they get frustrated and probably obstreperous.

This is especially an issue as the parents grow older, since they cannot go out and about as much as might be desirable. One father in his late seventies, finding that his son liked staying in the hostel, notes:

> You see, when he comes home, he sits there. I perhaps doze off in the chair, Mum perhaps has a cat nap, and William's got no friends, got no mates, nobody to have a laugh and a giggle with, you know? And I wonder whether he gets a little bit fed up.

It must be added that there is a common tendency to duck this question, to avoid facing up to it. Many, many parents feel that they never really made a decision on this matter, but simply 'jogged along' from day to day. There is no reason to change things when everything is all right: 'At the moment, she has a very happy life and I don't see any reason to change that.' Another mother puts it this way:

> I suppose, really, you always hope that things will improve. Perhaps the fits would improve. You just go on hoping that you can cope. Just thinking 'Oh, well, it'll be all right. We're managing all right.'. . . You don't do anything about it and you drift on a bit longer. It's always easier not to do anything about it, isn't it?

The reluctance to 'let go', then, derives from a very complex set of emotions. These are not always easy to unravel and are, in any case, heavily interrelated. Indeed, they commonly serve to reinforce each other. A sense of protectiveness, for instance, feeds the sense of responsibility, and where no obvious alternative is seen and no pressure felt to change course, the parent continues to feel protective and the son or daughter remains at home. Furthermore, as parents become increasingly accustomed to their situation, they can become almost reliant on it, adding to the reluctance to change.

But there are some parents who are very concerned to 'let go'. Some have plans to do so. Others suggest there is no point in giving seroius attention to this question because there is nowhere for their son or daughter to go. These are often parents of severely handicapped sons and daughters, for whom it is difficult to find short-term care, let alone help in the long term. Some feel very distressed about this issue, angry at the lack of opportunity and worried about whether they will ever find a place:

> If we were assured that wherever he went, he'd be accepted and there'd be no problems ... we'd be delighted. It's so important that he should actually break from us and that we should be able to have a life, as it were, without Steven. If only a place could be found, we'd be over the moon.

'After we're gone'

The worry about 'what will happen after I'm gone?' has rightly come to be seen as one of the deepest concerns of all parents of handicapped children. It is something parents think about from a very early age, the concern increasing as they see themselves growing older: 'Something's going to happen. We've got to get older. I wouldn't want it to happen that there was only one left here. To make that decision would be harder than it is now.' Some begin to look around and talk to other parents about what they will do, but there are many more who find it difficult to discuss the problem with people outside the home.

The older the parent, of course, the closer this worry is to the surface. Their own vulnerability becomes increasingly evident. As one widow notes: 'Now there's only me. I hate to feel that she's going to face the world alone.... Since I lost my husband, I've realized how uncertain everything is.' The concern to get things settled consequently becomes much stronger; in the words of a 75-year-old mother:

> If I knew what was going to happen to my child, I shouldn't worry about dying. If I could just know, if I could just have it in writing: 'Now, Mrs. Brown, when you're gone, your child will be taken care of.' If I just knew that, it's all I would want to know.

A number of parents talk about being able to 'die happy' if they were only satisfied about the arrangements made.

Where some plan is finally established, even if it is not able to be implemented immediately, there can be a very strong sense of relief. On learning that a place had been found for her daughter, for instance, one elderly mother notes:

> I felt so lightened. It lifted a worry off me...I'm not frightened to die. I mean, I've had a good life. And I know you can't look forward too far, can you, when you're getting older.... This is all you're thinking about, really. You're trying to see the end product of what's going to happen to your child.

But how do parents come to the point of thinking seriously about the future? For many, it is a long and slow process, the realization that something needs to be done building up over time. While parents frequently say that it is a subject which worries them from the time their son or daughter is very young, it is also one which many avoid confronting: 'From childhood, from babyhood, you think about it. But it's not pressing, is it? You know – well, you think you know – you've got a long lease on life.' No one likes to think about his or her own death. Furthermore, some are uncertain about where to go for any information. Some parents are reluctant to raise the subject with anyone in authority. In some households, the husband and wife never discuss the issue together, although each is worrying about it independently for years: 'it is a dreary subject; we don't talk about that kind of thing.'

One consequence of this tendency to avoid the issue is the slow development over time of an assumption that nothing will be done, that life will continue in the same pattern right to the end. They expect 'to live from day to day' or 'to take each day as it comes'. With no evident time presenting itself for making the break, or even considering the idea, a sense of inertia tends to take over: 'When you're happy together, there's lots of things you don't think about, really. I mean, because at the moment, we've just the four of us, we're quite happy.' Older parents often regret the lack of discussions many years before, which would have enabled them to break out of the mould in which they now find themselves.

One problem is that, compared to the expectations for their other children, the future is seen to be generally bleak:

> With ordinary families, your children ... get jobs and then they get married, don't they? You're happy for them. But this is so different. You can't feel happy for them because eventually you'll be gone and, well, you hope for the best.

It is also a matter of who will *care about* their son or daughter; another mother speaks about seeing a non-handicapped child get married: 'They are going to be capable of looking after themselves and you are entrusting your child into the hands of somebody else who does care.' The sense of permanency about the future, compared to short-term living away, can seem a real worry:

> It's going to be different because she's not coming back. It's going to be different because she's going to live there permanently. It's not a holiday and eventually that's going to sink into her little mind. ... No one's ever going to convince me otherwise. Whatever happens it's going to be the most terrible time of her life when I'm gone. I'm quite sure of that.

There are some parents who feel their situation is so hopeless that their only plan for the future is a hope that their son or daughter will die first or that they will die together. As one 75-year-old widow says: 'It's only now I keep thinking, oh, Martha, I hope I don't die before you. I hope we die together. That's the only thing.' Some parents suggest they would seriously consider 'taking my son with me' if they knew the end was near. This is in no way said lightly; the lack of any suitable place where someone would care for their son or daughter as they have is the source of real despair. It is not simply a matter of finding a place; it is a question of feeling that someone will devote themselves to the son or daughter, giving him or her love and proper care and protection. Here is one mother's reaction to a bad experience of her son in a hostel on a short-term basis:

> It was so desolate. ... I don't feel suicidal – I'm not the type –

but that was as near as I ever felt. I thought, God, I would rather take my child's life – I really mean this, I felt so strongly – than let him go into a place like that.

Keeping care in the family

In some families, the future plan for the mentally handicapped son or daughter has been set by the assumption that it is solely a family matter. This is, perhaps, the more traditional way, of families looking after their own. Parents thus expect other relatives to take over, most commonly another son or daughter. Very little is known about what brothers and sisters feel about taking on the responsibility for their handicapped sibling, either before it actually happens or afterwards. Many are heavily involved in helping with the day-to-day care over the years, if only because they provide a spare pair of hands. It is evident that some are brought up from an early age both to expect that they will carry on when their parents cannot cope and to believe that it is right that they do so. They are, in a sense, groomed for the job. Some parents discuss this issue with the relevant son or daughter and feel assured that he or she will take on the necessary care.

But this question is also the source of considerable tension in some families. Much of this is undiscussed and unresolved. A number of parents say they would like another son or daughter to take over when they can no longer cope, but never seem to find the right time to raise the issue for serious discussion:

> Well, now, that is something that we haven't gone that deeply into. It's just been said, 'Oh, don't have any worries about what will happen . . . we'd always look after him.' I suppose we never got round to discussing that.

Others say that another son or daughter has agreed to take on the necessary care, but express some uncertainty about whether he or she will do so when the time comes. Furthermore, the ability or willingness of the son's or daughter's spouse to cope with the necessary demands is sometimes called into question. A number of uneasy explanations are often put forward: 'They lead very busy lives . . . and they just haven't time.' Parents are very hesitant to press and know that, in the end, it will be up to the son or daughter to decide: 'You can't legislate from the grave.'

Much more common, however, are the parents who feel they do

not want the responsibility to pass on to another son or daughter. They are all too familiar with the restrictions which a handicapped person imposes on a family and do not want their other children to have to bear these on a permanent basis. Parents often suggest that their other children have done enough during their period in the household and deserve a bit of freedom. There is also concern that living together would bring unnecessary friction and, in the words of one mother, 'they would grow to dislike her'. The responsibility for a handicapped person is seen as one for parents, but not for a brother or sister: 'There's no way we'd want to put it on our other children, you know, to give them the worry.... They've got their own lives, haven't they ... it wouldn't be fair on them.'

CHAPTER 4

The Problem of Independence

The biggest enemies the mentally handicapped have got are their parents. . . . Over-protective. Won't let them go, won't let them make their own mistakes. I've realized this for many years and fought against it and that's why we've taken so many chances with Stuart.

Father of Stuart, aged 31

One crucial aspect of accepting that any son or daughter can leave home is the development of independence. No parent would wish their child to leave home until he or she was able to do so with some assurance. There is a need not only to teach a number of key skills but also to develop sufficient emotional disengagement for a son or daughter to cope on his or her own. These issues are not essentially different for parents whose son or daughter has a mental handicap, but there is a very critical difference in their circumstances. The experience of caring for a handicapped child over the years creates a great sense of protectiveness. This, in turn, can considerably hamper the development of independence.

Protective parents

For any parent, there is an inevitable conflict between the wish to protect a child from harm and the concern to teach all the necessary skills to cope with day-to-day life. This begins from the moment a small toddler is first able to explore the world for himself and continues, on a different level, right into adulthood. It ranges from the practical problems of handling a knife or crossing the road to the more complex problems of human relationships. There is no simple way of knowing when a child is ready to use the oven, go to the shops on his own, or spend a night away. Each parent has to decide when the benefits from allowing a bit more independence outweigh the risks which may be incurred. These issues, indeed, are often the subject of considerable arguments within families, not only between parents and child but also between husband and wife.

All of these problems are also faced by parents whose son or daughter has a mental handicap. Their child, too, can learn, although he or she may not do so as quickly or as early as other children. But the context in which such questions are considered by parents is entirely different. The experiences of bringing up a handicapped son or daughter, coupled with comments from others outside the home, conspire to make parents very protective. Not surprisingly, many avoid all risks.

Practical tasks

What does this mean in practice? It means that parents feel unable to devolve much responsibility onto their son or daughter. Faced with the problem of risk, combined with uncertainty about whether any message has 'got through', many do not teach even simple household chores. One mother explains:

> Oh, no, I won't let her use the kettle, make tea. Oh, no. I won't let her do anything like that because I'm frightened she'll burn herself. The only thing she does do, she went out with her cup and poured herself some more tea while the water was in the kettle.... I won't let her do ironing. Nothing like that. I just won't let her. She probably could, but I just won't let her. I won't take the chance.

There is little doubt that the very existence of a handicap makes parents feel protective. This derives in part from a natural tendency among parents to protect any child. Since in the case of a handicapped son or daughter, the vulnerability does not diminish as quickly, the protectiveness also continues. In the words of one mother:

> I suppose a mother always has that protective instinct with

all her kids. But as they get older, you realize, don't you, that they can care for themselves; they can shoulder their own responsibilities. Well, I've always had the feeling that George never could.

But such protectiveness also arises because of the special vulnerability of a person with a handicap. Parents feel they have to be especially careful over the years:

> It sort of grows with you. You've had to do so much for them, training and teaching them when they're small, because they don't learn as quickly as other children. You sort of take care of them and that's how it goes. It grows with you, you see.

As mentioned in an earlier chapter, parents find it difficult to see their son or daughter, whatever his or her age, as an adult: 'Maybe I'm doing things for her as a child and I ought to be doing things for her as an adult. I've never thought about it like that.' Where the handicap is particularly severe, this can be carried to an even greater extreme, with the son or daughter viewed as a 'baby'. Given the capabilities, this is not always surprising; as one father explains:

> She's never grown up. And that's how we look at it. That is the only way that you can look at her. Her mind has not matured, so in other words, we've had a baby. We've had to nurse her and had to feed her, toilet her, dress her, undress her, bath her. It's only what you do with a newborn baby.

There is also a tendency to try to compensate their son or daughter for the existence of a handicap. Parents give 'that bit more' to their son or daughter 'because you think, "that's my boy, what else has he got in life?" '. There is also a willingness to stand up for the handicapped child against the others; one father explains; 'You'll fight for them even against his own brothers. And they begin to know it.' All of this, of course, increases the handicapped son's or daughter's feeling of protectedness and the parents' increasing need to protect.

This feeling sometimes arises from parents' sense of guilt in having given birth to a child with a handicap. In the words of one mother:

> We're over-compensating, I suppose. What it comes down

to is guilt. We feel guilty that we have somehow caused this child to be leading a far from perfect life. . . . My common sense tells me that it's not my fault, but you are never free of the feeling that your child will never lead the sort of life you wanted for her and you grieve for her because of that.

Comments from outside

Parents' tendency to protectiveness is easily reinforced by thoughtless comments from others. Many have had some experience with neighbours or other local people, who do not understand the nature of mental handicap and therefore cause some problem for their son or daughter. But perhaps of greater significance is a poor experience with a professional person. This often begins at a very early stage, when the child is born or has been diagnosed as having a handicap. Well-meaning doctors who suggest that parents 'go home and forget him', for instance, create a well of mistrust: 'They just said he was a Mongol baby and he'd never be any good. As blunt as that.' Another mother, whose son's handicap was diagnosed considerably later, provides a similar story:

> I was told to forget him, more or less, that he was ineducable and I couldn't do anything with him. They said the best thing was to get on with our own lives. Well, I didn't accept that.

Parents are left with the feeling that the world of professionals does not take their child seriously.

Remarks made later in life create particular damage. These may be offered with genuine sympathy, but with little understanding of what parents feel. A moment of crisis is often the source of some professional intervention. One couple, when their daughter was critically ill, had brought a locum doctor to the house: 'The doctor said, "the cross you've been bearing so long will soon be lifted". [My husband] told him to get out and not come back.' A mother, on the death of her husband, found herself shocked that the vicar should suggest that she find another home for her daughter. The resolve of these parents to protect their child needs no underlining.

This issue can also arise when parents begin to inquire about alternative care, either on a short-term basis or for the longer term future. This is a period of great sensitivity, with parents looking out for any indication that their son or daughter will not be treated well. One mother notes: 'We got talking [with the social worker] and she says, "oh, don't worry", she says, "when anything ails you, they'll put her in a hostel". You know, quite blunt.' The impact of such off-hand remarks is incredibly strong.

Too much affection

Their own tendency to protectiveness is one about which many parents express considerable guilt. They talk of their feeling of having failed their child, although perhaps for the best of reasons: '... because as parents we gave him too much affection and not enough, shall we say, stricture.' It is also an issue over which there can be a great deal of conflict, both between parents and the outside world and between parents themselves. One mother, arguing against the pressures on parents to make their children more independent, puts it this way:

> Other people seem to have this thing that they've got to be independent. I don't agree, I don't agree at all. . . . I think they make too much of it, because you can cause a lot of heartache by pushing someone who can't do it.

The intra-family problem is even more common: 'My husband says to me, "he's grown up, he's a man, you mustn't treat him as a boy". But that's one thing to say and another to do after all these years. . . . We have been at loggerheads sometimes.'

There are some parents, however, who make a virtue out of their situation, who feel that their own need to be protective is in the best interests of their child. They point out the worries of other parents over drugs and other kinds of problems:

> In a world like this, I would have hated her to be normal. And left home and got into trouble and all that. . . . No, she's protected here. A blessing. A blessing having a child like that in the world as it is today.

Of course, any lack of teaching is not solely a matter of parental protectiveness. Parents also find themselves with diminishing patience with the tasks they need to teach. It can be exhausting trying to teach a handicapped child a new skill; many parents become discouraged and decide not to bother or not to try as hard as they think they should. It is difficult to watch a child struggle to put his clothes on, and tiresome to re-sew buttons again and again.

Some parents simply become tired of arguments:

> I'd have liked him to have become more independent. I suppose it's my own fault. I should have been firmer with him, shouldn't I?... You've got to get them in a really happy frame of mind, but all the time he needs reassurance.

Whatever the job, it simply becomes easier for parents to do it themselves.

Furthermore, the wish to protect cannot be dismissed lightly. Many parents know of accidents involving handicapped children and some have experience themselves. One, whose daughter had been knocked down by a car, explains: 'She couldn't think quick enough to cross the road. It's always frightened me after that. An experience like that leaves a sting.' A number of handicaps themselves stem from accidents, not only with traffic but from falls or severe burns in the home. Most parents know of some time when they could have been more careful; having to live with the consequences, it is not surprising that they are cautious.

Many parents find that their sons and daughters are said to be much more capable when outside the parental home. This is a two-edged sword for parents: a mixture of pleasure that they can do it, combined with a sense of failure that it does not happen at home. Parents are often put under pressure to get the same results at home, such as this mother whose son was said to be very helpful at his Centre:

> My son washes up there and he does all these things, and you know each time they've said this, it's made me feel that I've failed him somewhere.... So I've really been patient when he's got home [but] between picking up the cloth and the cup, he's forgotten what he was going to do.

This, of course, is no different from most families where children are found to be helpful when visiting relatives or friends, but are reluctant to help out in their own home.

Relating to other people

All of this discussion has centred on the relatively easy side to bringing up a child: teaching practical skills. Much more difficult is the whole business of teaching children how to cope with and relate to other people. This becomes especially problematic as sons and daughters grow into active adolescents, eager to adopt the life styles they see around them. Parents suddenly have to cope with attitudes to alcohol and drugs, appropriate relationships and, of course, sex. These problems also affect parents whose son or daughter has a mental handicap. Where the handicap is fairly mild, the issues are not so different from those facing all parents. For parents whose son's or daughter's handicap is more severe, or who has been heavily protected at home, the lack of exposure to some of the issues makes their situation quite different. All parents seem concerned, however, to find the right balance.

The problem of friendship, both with members of the same sex and with members of the opposite sex, proves to be an issue with many families. Parents note that their son or daughter has a 'little boyfriend' but commonly do not view it as a very serious matter: 'He's got a girlfriend that drives us mad. He's got an absolute crush on a girl; there's nothing sexual about it. But he takes cakes from here and buys her presents. She won't respond.' Parents get somewhat more concerned when there is talk of marriage. This seems to occur particularly with daughters, who talk about the wedding they would like to have, perhaps sparked off by the thrill of a sister's marriage.

Developing independence is not solely about sex and marriage, however. There are many questions concerning the amount of freedom a son or daughter is given – where he or she can go and when – which are likely to be experienced by parents of any adolescent. Parents of handicapped sons and daughters feel they have even more to fear, because of their greater vulnerability. Many worry deeply about the risks to which their son or daughter might be exposed and their fear of trouble:

> I've probably been pretty strict with her because I've been terrified of anything going wrong with her. I didn't want her getting to the point where she was allowed to go out on her own and make her own friends and [get] into trouble. . . . I didn't like the idea of her smoking and going in pubs and mixing with every Tom, Dick and Harry. She is easily led.

Parents also worry about living with themselves if something did go wrong: 'I'd feel that I'd let him down. I'd let him go out and he'd got into this mess or trouble, whatever it was, and I'd feel so guilty. I'd think, "well, that would never have happened but for me letting him go off."'

In some families, it becomes a vicious circle. If the handicapped child is not taught, it follows that he or she does not learn and therefore becomes more defenceless and less capable of managing in a variety of difficult circumstances. As he or she grows older, the parents become more protective, sensing the inability to cope with either practical activities inside the home or a range of hazards outside it. The early protectiveness, in their own words, spawns an even greater need to be protective.

Developing skills and taking risks

Not all parents are over-protective of their sons and daughters. There are many families who go to enormous trouble to teach their handicapped child. They see this as crucial to their son's or daughter's development and ability to manage in the world: 'What we call common sense, they haven't got and your first teaching is teach what you can of self-preservation'. This is partly a question of teaching some simple understanding of how to cope with the hazards of life. But it is also a matter of teaching basic living skills. In comparison to parents of non-handicapped children, the problems are greater because of the greater difficulty experienced by the son or daughter. Here is a mother of a mildly handicapped son, slightly paralysed on one side:

> When he started growing up, he found it difficult to do buttons up, you know, with one hand, and shoe laces. It was sheer agony to sit and watch him. But he'd done it. I don't think he would have . . . if we hadn't sat back.

Sometimes the parents' urge to teach stems from the unwillingness of anyone else to do so. This was especially the case many years ago, when mentally handicapped children were declared to be ineducable. Many parents fought long and hard to prove the authorities wrong. One mother of a son, who was said as a small child to be incapable of learning, describes how she persevered:

> He didn't know his colours and my reaction was, when the other children were having their afternoon nap, to concentrate on him with his bricks. I taught him his colours. It took me three days, but I proved to myself that he was teachable and I went on from there.

Indeed, the same mother continues:

I developed his own personality myself; I thought that was important... I thought he had a right to be a person in his own right – that's how I looked at it. And he is, he's definitely a character.

The problem of risk

In the course of such learning, the handicapped sons and daughters are necessarily exposed to some risk. This is perhaps nowhere more true than where parents let them explore the neighbourhood alone. Yet many parents feel that it is important to give their son or daughter this freedom. One mother of a severely handicapped and epileptic daughter, for instance, describes how she followed behind her daughter, to see how she managed:

A few weeks ago, she said, 'I want to go to the library on my own.' Now, that means crossing a very busy road. She wanted to do it... so I tailed her on the other side of the road. There's no way I could let her go on her own, but she didn't know I was there.

One father, also giving his son considerable freedom to explore, notes one of the problems: 'One Saturday morning, we'll say to him, "look, you go and see your brother", which is a fair distance.... His brother might be out and he takes himself off. He may be an hour or so late.' All such activity forms part of the slow learning process.

Many parents take great pride in their son's or daughter's achievements. One father describes what it means for a handicapped person to achieve certain skills:

I'm extremely proud of her. I'm proud of her accomplishments, all of them.... It costs them a far greater effort to learn to do everything: washing, cleaning their teeth, dressing, feeding themselves. It's a much bigger effort for them than it is for you or I, and we would do well to remember that.

And here is the mother of a daughter in her late 20s with Down's Syndrome:

I've taught her. The first thing I taught her not to be afraid of the iron. How to work it. She's perfectly normal as far as that. I've taught her how to bake, she's a beautiful baker, she can beat me at pastry. I taught her all that, you see. When you give them faith in themselves and say 'you can do it, course you can do it' – she'll do it. . . . These children need an awful lot of help. I mean, to say 'go and do that' – that's not good. Patience is the most important thing.

Parents are often quite pleased as well at the strides made by their son or daughter through other means. This may be through exposure to new friends or through their day centre or other daytime activity:

Everyone's seen a difference in him. I mean, he'll sit and have a conversation with you now, which he never used to do. I'm sure it's down to the help he's having at the training centre. They're absolutely marvellous.

Many parents feel, however, that they gain little social approval for exposing their son or daughter to risk. As one father says:

Some of our friends have been horrified at the risks and the freedoms we gave John, but the consequence is that some of their children . . . although they're basically less handicapped, they never go out on their own, they've got no understanding of money and have got very few social graces.

A mother, also encouraging her daughter to learn, puts the matter this way: 'I think this is important for her. Not for me, but for her. And I feel she'll have a better chance in life if she can stand up and do these things and be a help. She won't be pushed aside.'

Trial separations

One means by which greater independence is fostered for many handicapped sons and daughters is through temporary stays away from home. There are a number of ways in which these can occur. Sometimes a relative, including a sibling who has moved out of the home, may invite the handicapped person to stay for one night or longer. Day centres, as well as voluntary organizations, often organize holidays for a week or two. Many hostels, essentially providing long-term care, also have facilities for short-stays, often intended primarily 'to give the parents a break'.

Whatever the ostensible purpose of these separations, they can

serve a very important function in enabling handicapped people to
learn to cope outside the home. Indeed, they can be seen to form
part of a programme for preparing sons and daughters for leaving
home. Parents themselves are often well aware of the need to
develop this independence, particularly where they are themselves
inclined to be over protective:

> Well, to be quite honest it would make him more
> independent than what he is now.... I mean, he would have
> to cook his meals, have to make his bed. Whereas when
> they're at home, that's what mums are for.

Other mothers recognize the need for emotional distancing, as one
mother put it 'weaning him from me'.

At the same time, and perhaps even more critically, these
separations also enable parents to become accustomed to life
without their son or daughter. Many need, as they themselves
admit, to wean themselves from their child. Where the parental
tie is particularly close, and has developed over a long period of
time, this can be very difficult. Every parent knows the feeling of
an empty house when a child is away. How much more difficult
when that child has been part of the household for a very long
time.

Some parents describe missing their son or daughter in very
physical terms. Here is the mother of a son in his late 20s:

> When Edward isn't there, and he isn't sat in that chair – he
> always sat in that one chair – it looks so empty, you know....
> It just feels as if you've lost your whole life, you know.
> Everything seems to be empty in the house when he isn't sat
> in that chair.

Others point out the loss of their own role, the feeling of having
too much freedom: as one puts it rather vividly, 'you've lost an
anchor'. One mother goes on to explain: 'You feel as though
you've nothing to do. I mean, he takes that much looking after, he
needs all your attention. You've to dress him, you've to put him on
the toilet ... and you've nothing like that to do.'

The first few times a son or daughter goes away are particularly
critical: 'When Alan goes away he's always on our minds....
You're never free, you know, you're always thinking, "I wonder
what he's doing? I wonder if he's all right?"' The urge to check up,

to find out how things are going, as with any parent during a child's first stay away from home, is very strong. As one father explains: 'My wife worries a lot when he's there. As a matter of fact, she's phoning up before he gets there.' Parents not only worry about how their son or daughter will cope but also about whether he or she will be able to communicate his or her needs to others.

Where parents have experienced separation, however, and found that their son or daughter was well looked after, their attitude can change dramatically. They find they can relax, can begin to enjoy the time on their own and turn their attention to their other children or to other interests entirely. Many experience an enormous feeling of relief. This is partly the physical relief of not having to carry out their usual day-to-day chores. But it is also a relief that someone else is capable of looking after their son or daughter, that they are not, after all, indispensable: 'In all honesty, I feel great. You know, I feel like it's a big load lifted off my shoulders... a lot of tensions all gone.'

Of course, where the experience outside the home is not successful, the opposite reaction can occur. Sometimes it is simply that the son or daughter did not mix well and came home unhappy. In others, parents feel that there has been clear evidence of neglect, for instance forgetting to dispense crucial medicine. Parents can come to feel that they are even more needed and that the outside world is even less to be trusted. As noted in the preceding chapter, this is a common source of parents' feelings of sole responsibility and an unwillingness to let go.

The experience of separation is important for the development of independence in all relationships. Non-handicapped children learn that they can manage on their own through experience of going away from home, first for a night and later over longer periods. Their parents, too, need to learn that their children can cope outside their home. This is a question of realizing that the physical needs can be provided by others, as well as themselves, and that emotional involvement does not necessarily require day-to-day proximity. These issues are no different in the case of handicapped sons and daughters, except that their needs for care may be greater. In both cases, separations are an important component in the development of independence.

Independence in other families

In fact, the broad problem of developing independence for handicapped sons and daughters is paralleled for parents of all children, as has been noted. But differences arise in two important ways. First, there is the lack of initiative from the handicapped son or daughter to break away from the parent. This is probably partly due to a passivity developed over the years and partly to a lack of opportunity to do anything else. Parents of non-handicapped children do not have to think about these problems, as they are thrust on them, often quite forceably. Their growing children not only try to take on activities involving physical independence but also find their own friends and relationships. Indeed, the decision to marry and form a new family is often seen as the key indicator of full maturity and independence. In the case of handicapped sons and daughters, in contrast, it is the parents who have to make the running. It is not an easy task.

A second difference concerns the value which parents place on their children achieving maturity. However difficult the process of letting go, parents usually take some pride in watching their children grow up and become adult. They recognize the need for their children to express preferences, make their own decisions and eventually take independent action. Indeed, the lack of such behaviour among young adults can be the cause of some concern to parents. For mentally handicapped young people, in contrast, there is almost inevitably a lower parental expectation of developing maturity. Perhaps as a consequence, similar behaviours do not appear to be valued in a similar way. Parents may fail to acknowledge – or may even dismiss – any adult choices the handicapped person wishes to make, for instance, having a boyfriend or girlfriend or wanting 'a place of my own'. While parents may have some reason in seeing these choices as inappropriate, the process does little to encourage the mentally handicapped person to develop independence of thought or action.

CHAPTER 5

Looking at the Alternatives

> A house with normal house furniture... a sort of place that becomes home. With the atmosphere which he grew up in, with friends from school or friends from work there. Where people remembered it was his birthday, where the people there would genuinely care for him.
>
> Mother of Sam, aged 18

Sam's mother is describing what she would wish a future home for her severely handicapped son to be like. In sentiment, if not in detail, her description is echoed by many other parents. Indeed, what parent, when thinking about a future home for a teenage son or daughter would not agree that these quite modest features are desirable? But for parents whose son or daughter has a mental handicap, there are some differences. Their sons and daughters are unlikely to be able to go and set up such a home for themselves. The parents are therefore much more heavily involved in the choice of any future home, assuming that a move takes place at all. The question of a move from home is not simply about undergoing painful processes of separation; there are real questions about where the son or daughter can go. The options available may well influence the decision to make the break. There is a need to look at parents' views on these questions.

What parents want

When parents describe the kind of living arrangements they would like to see available for their son or daughter, one characteristic is always mentioned. It must be a *home* – not an institution, not a hostel, not a boarding house, but a *home*. This feature transcends all others and underpins virtually all other requirements. It is important therefore to consider the qualities a home is seen to have.

In parents' eyes, a home has three core qualities all of which are concerned with a need for *care*. It should provide love and affection, an understanding of individual needs and a rooted sense of belonging. The importance of these would probably be agreed by the parent of any adult child, but their need becomes greater when that child has a handicap. Parents' natural feelings of love and protection are even stronger in the face of the added vulnerability arising from a handicap. The idea that their son or daughter might live in an environment where he or she might be unloved, misunderstood or unwanted is simply unbearable.

Home is also associated with a sense of security. Parents differ, however, in the stress they place on different facets of security or protection. To some, it is primarily a matter of safety; they want to minimize the possibility of physical risk. Others emphasize the need for an emotionally secure environment. They see this as one in which there is stability, support and no likelihood of abuse or maltreatment. In its more extreme forms, this requirement restricts the search for a home to one which is not exposed to any of the harms or hardships of the 'real' world.

Permanency is another aspect of care which parents associate with home. They dislike the idea of transience and want any placement to be reasonably long term. This is partly because they want to see their son or daughter settled, to have some knowledge of where he or she will be living. But it is also because they feel that familiarity of surroundings is important to their son or daughter and that any change could be quite disruptive.

These needs for a caring, secure and permanent environment are fundamental to parents' requirements of any future home for their son or daughter. It is hardly surprising. They, after all, have provided this kind of home for their son or daughter, not only in childhood, but well into adulthood. There can be no possibility that they might 'put them away' or 'farm them out' to somewhere which did not hold these qualities.

Creating a home

How, then, can the qualities of a home be created in residential care for people with mental handicaps? What is it that provides the homely environment that parents so much want to see? There are a number of determining features on which parents are largely agreed.

Small in size

One of the most central issues is that of size. Parents seek homes which are small – perhaps six to eight residents, certainly no more then ten or twelve. As one parent questions: 'How can you create a home when there are 20 or 30 people living there?' A small home is important for a number of reasons. Perhaps the most essential is that it will help to ensure individual attention. The smaller the home, the greater the likelihood that personal needs will be met and that their son or daughter will not be neglected or overlooked: 'I think Michael would get lost if there were a lot of people around – just probably blend into the background and he wouldn't get noticed. Whereas, in a smaller unit he'd be more of an individual.'

In some cases this is a worry about physical neglect – that no one will make sure they brush their teeth, or wash themselves properly or have clean and well pressed clothes. But in others, the concern is about some understanding of psychological and emotional needs. Parents want to be sure that someone would notice if their son or daughter was bored, lonely, unhappy or simply wanted a cuddle.

There is also concern about the opportunity of getting to know other people well. The smaller the number of people, the greater the likelihood that their son or daughter will find personal companionship and support:

> If there's, say, three or four of them together they can bring each other on, they encourage each other, they do little things for each other. One can do this, one can't do that, so all right they help each other.... Now my daughter has difficulty with her zips, and her pal has difficulty with buttons, so Elaine does her buttons, this little girl does zips, you see. And if they can get in that sort of atmosphere where they're helping each other...

Much of the discussion of size revolves around a wish to create a 'family atmosphere': 'I like the idea – a little group with six of them. She's got somebody there with her ... and she'll not be on her own. I think they are like a little close-knit family.' In essence, a 'little close-knit family' is what most parents are trying to attain. In their eyes, that is natural and what their son or daughter is most used to. A much larger setting will not only be unfamiliar to their son or daughter but also disconcerting.

A homely atmosphere

Creating a family atmosphere means giving handicapped people a sense that they are accepted – accepted for who they are and what they do: 'It's somewhere to come home to relax. . . . It's somewhere where they can feel comfortable and safe.' Related to this is the issue of freedom – freedom to be themselves and, within limits, do what they want to do. Although many parents seek some supervision, they do not want this to quell the choices that their son or daughter can express. One mother sums up the view of many:

> Somewhere where he could have all his familiar things around him. You know, be able to watch the television, the programmes that he likes. Just the ordinary things like food. . . . Well, a second home – that's what I'm trying to describe, aren't I?

A 'second home' is precisely what most parents are trying to describe. And, whatever their sons' and daughters' individual behaviour or preferences, parents feel that they, like everyone else, should be allowed to experience the comfort and privacy of their own home.

Underlying many of these comments, of course, is a strong distaste for any form of institutionalization. As one father puts it:

> There comes a point where, however well run the place is, and however well meaning people are, the sheer size of the thing turns it into an institution rather than a group. And, I think you *must* keep that idea of a group.

Such views are often expressed in full recognition of the cost implications entailed; the need to avoid any aspect of institutionalization is seen to be overriding.

Parents also feel that a home-like atmosphere should be created through the nature of the accommodation and its furnishings. Residential care should *look* like a home as well as *be* one. For some, this makes the use of ordinary domestic housing essential. Others believe, however, that this aim can be achieved by building domestic units within a larger complex. Of particular importance in this context is the bedroom. Most parents feel that their son or daughter should have a room of his or her own, or at the very most, shared only with a close friend. As one father says: 'Everyone should have a room of their own in my opinion.'

The need of one's own room is not simply for privacy. Handicapped people need to 'have all their own things and do what they like in their own room.' But this is also important to develop a son's or daughter's feeling of independence. As one mother explains:

> A private bedroom [is important] so that she can feel she is an individual. Dormitories are all right for people who have an independence within themselves, but for someone like Tracy, the independence has to be matured. And if you're going to make her independent then she has to feel she is an individual.

Many parents also seek some *proximity* to their own home, so that visits can be made (both ways) without too much inconvenience: 'I want her near me. I don't want her to go too far away that I don't see her.' Sometimes this is put in terms of proximity to married brothers or sisters living nearby, so that they, too, especially in the long term, can easily keep in touch. As one mother says, 'Where, perhaps, after dinner they would say, "we could go and get Jill" – it wouldn't have to be an upheaval or a day's outing or anything.'

Staffing and supervision

Most important, however, are the people who will help to create the caring and homely environment – the staff. Most parents cannot envisage that their son or daughter might live somewhere where there are no residential staff. Even those few who feel their son or daughter to be capable of living reasonably independently stress the importance of some close supervision.

What kind of people do parents want these staff to be? It is not without significance that parents often describe them as 'house mothers' and 'house fathers'. Indeed, what many parents seek is some kind of replica of themselves. This is not arrogance; it is simply that the role and qualities of staff parallel the parental role. Parents constantly note the same attributes: 'loving', 'caring', 'understanding', 'dedicated', 'patient', and many similar virtues. Here is a group of parents, discussing the qualities they want in staff:

> 'They must care – care about what they're doing.'
> 'You must have ordinary people with an interest for the kids.'
> 'And a hell of a lot of patience.'
> 'You've got to give them love that's the main thing.'
> 'They've got to be devoted to what they're doing.'
> 'Anyone of us here, you know, who have handicapped children – that would be the ideal situation.'

In general, parents are much more concerned about the personal qualities of staff than about professional training or qualifications: 'It's imaginative care, really. It doesn't matter what letters they've got after their name.' This does not mean that they do not have a long list of qualities they *do* require:

> It's nothing to do with qualifications, basically, either some people have it or they don't. Some people can work with these youngsters and some people find it very difficult. . . . You've got to be very, very optimistic and outgoing really, not easily discouraged. And I think you've got to have a terrific sense of humour, you've got to be able to jolly people along and keep cheerful. And you've got to be very determined and not take 'no' for an answer. And you've got to be good at establishing good relations on a permanent basis and be consistent . . . . But it helps if you have skills as well – skills for them to be able to learn things. We've noticed again and again, even with the most professional sorts of people, how they tend to ignore the non-speaking person. They don't talk to them except to direct them, which is very, very sad.

A few parents, primarily those with severely handicapped sons or daughters, feel some training in nursing is important. But even they do not consider nursing qualifications alone to be sufficient. It is the personal qualities of the people who provide care that transform any kind of residential care into a 'home'.

Some controversial issues

Although parents are largely agreed about the essential qualities of alternative care, there are some differences in their views about the exact form in which it should be provided. Some seek what they call 'family style homes'; some, units within hostels; some, sheltered accommodation; some, village communities, and so forth. Throughout all these different forms of care, the idea of a small, home-like unit remains a constant. But there are some differences of principle which need an airing.

Segregation or integration

First, there is the question of whether people with a mental handicap should be segregated in special complexes or communities or whether they should live in ordinary houses, in ordinary streets, in an ordinary way. Parents are quite divided about this issue. On the one hand there are some who feel that integration is essential. They see this as important for their son's or daughter's development:

> When you're talking about complexes I think there's a danger of them being too cossetted and they don't see anybody other than their own kind and I think there should be a lot of contact with 'normal' people, because I think they could go back instead of forward. Because a lot of these people there's the potential and I don't think they'd improve if they were just kept amongst their own kind all the time.

Parents who hold this view also tend to argue for more education of the non-handicapped population, to overcome what they see as considerable prejudice against mentally handicapped people. Attitudes will only change, they suggest, through normal contact and communication. Indeed, 'special' communities are seen as abhorrent not only because it is alien to 'shut them away' but also because they reinforce fears about the danger or abnormality of people with handicaps.

Other parents, however, hold a quite different view. They argue that mentally handicapped people need their own 'special environment', as they 'like living with people like themselves'. This view arises from a concern to protect the handicapped person from the wider community. A more segregated location enables them to be safe and protected:

> They'd be with the same sort of person, no outside people interfering with them a lot. I know some people would have to be there, but it would be their own sort of thing. . . . Outside people can be very very cruel. Even today, these days, you don't realize but they can be. They're not always accepted at places. But if they had a place of their own, they could work and live together.

Some parents, not surprisingly, are very ambivalent about this issue. On the one hand they want their sons and daughters to be protected within a sheltered environment. On the other, they want them to be accepted within the ordinary community. They therefore modify the requirement for a special community: 'Perhaps a large house, in its own grounds on the outskirts of a town where there is not too much traffic' or 'a community just outside a town or village where they can go to mix with the usual residents.'

Training for independence

A second controversial issue is whether mentally handicapped people should be given training to extend their ability to live independently. Relatively few parents believe that their son or daughter could be trained to live a fairly independent life. Those that do sometimes seek forms of care which might develop their son's or daughter's abilities and look to the more independent styles of hostels or homes. One mother explores the benefits of this kind of arrangement:

> They get a bit more independence. They more or less look after themselves. It's like a home. When they've been out all day, you come back and cook your own meal. . . . It makes them more independent.

Most parents feel that their son or daughter would need considerable preparation to be able to live this independently. Some suggest that other people, such as residential care workers, would probably prepare them better than they could.

More commonly, however, parents see considerable limits on the amount of independence which can be achieved and advocate a 'safety net' of services which need to be provided. They tend to argue that while mentally handicapped people, including their son or daughter, should be encouraged to do as much as possible for themselves, this should not be taken 'too far' by people expecting 'too much'. It is primarily an avoidance of risk which is at issue here. Louise's mother explains:

> At the training centre they do have a flat and they do make beans on toast and things like that – well I know Louise refuses point blank to cooperate in anything that involves cooking, because I've discouraged it. I got up one morning and my chip pan was on and she was standing peeling a potato. Now that potato could take one hour and a half to peel and chip – where would the chip pan have been? I've put a total ban on everything to do with bottles, cookers, the lot. A total ban. She would not cross the barrier of doing it at [the Centre]. The staff have asked me why and I said because I forbid it. . . . There is a limit to what you can expect them to do.

A few parents take the more extreme view that their son or daughter would not be capable of doing very much, whatever the environment. They argue that it would therefore be pointless for any kind of rehabilitative efforts to be made on their behalf. Some of these parents have a son or daughter with a very severe mental handicap, often with accompanying physical disabilities. But this is not invariably the case; even where the handicap is much less severe, parents often see no potential for development. Gerald, who is spastic but has only a mild mental handicap, is judged by his parents to be in this category:

> If I thought Gerald was capable of looking after himself, I wouldn't hesitate, but I know he isn't. He couldn't boil a kettle. He couldn't do anything like that. . . . There's [this idea] where people live together as a little family, if one can't do his shoe laces up, somebody does it for him. I mean this is helpful, but you're never independent, are you. You've always got to rely on someone, always.

Most parents, then, see training for independence as a good thing, but only up to a point. Part of their anxiety is related to safety and a strong desire to avoid any hint of risk. But some parents acknowledge that they may be somewhat too protective. When pressed, they wonder what their son or daughter might achieve, if given a more independent way of living. While they would be proud to see real development, they consider the stakes too high to take any risk.

Staffing levels

Finally, there is the issue of staffing levels. This is less controversial, as parents' views tend to depend on the severity of their son's or daughter's handicap. Where this is very severe, parents tend to be quite certain that there is a need for a high staffing ratio, to ensure constant personalized care, both during the day and at night. This is not simply to provide physical care but to ensure that their son or daughter gets some activity and stimulation. One mother explains:

> I need somewhere where I know she's going to get attention at night, I know she's going to get constant attention during the day. . . . When it's time for food, I would like to think that they are going to cut it up for her and it's going to be the sort of food she would like to eat. I'd like to think she was kept dry and she was able to make them understand what she wanted to do.

The need for a high level of staffing is not stated solely by parents whose son or daughter has a severe handicap. Even where the handicap is fairly mild, some parents consider it necessary to have meals and other services provided. Many parents see this as a continuation of their parental roles. Meals, washing and so forth are normally provided for the children in any home and since their sons or daughters are viewed as children, they consider it normal that such provision should be made. As one father explains:

> We're talking about a home. Where meals are provided and if he wants a snack he goes and makes a snack. We're talking about a home, so that facilities and services will apply as in a normal home.

This is part of what home is seen to be about.

Some judgements on what exists

To what extent do parents find that what they want is an option open to them? In other words, given that they know what they want, is their reluctance to move their son or daughter based on the limitations of what they see to be available? To what extent do they have experience of the existing provision?

There are two main types of residential accommodation widely available to people with a mental handicap. First, there are hostels and staffed homes, run either by local authorities, voluntary organizations or private bodies. They vary considerably in size, from as few as seven or eight people to as many as 40 residents, although some have smaller living units within them. Some are run on rehabilitative lines, preparing the more able residents for a move to independent accommodation. Others provide fully staffed accommodation with all the related services and are intended for long-term residence. Many of the larger hostels make some provision for short-term respite care.

Secondly, there are various types of independent accommodation, covering group homes, cluster flats and single accommodation units. These are run both by local authorities and other bodies. They involve people living, either individually or in groups, in ordinary housing. There are usually no resident staff, but regular supervision and support is generally provided either by field social workers or by residential care staff from nearby hostels or residential units.

In some areas, authorities make provision for fostering or 'family placement', whereby people with mental handicaps go to live with other families. Additionally, some local authorities buy places in homes outside their area. There are also various private arrangements, such as village communities, provided by particular trusts or foundations. But most parents believe that in reality their choices will be confined to local provision, unless they have plans for care to pass to another member of the family.

In the past, mental hospitals were a potential source of short- or long-term care for families, but this is changing. In line with government policy to promote community care, hospitals are no longer admitting many patients, other than urgent cases. The long-term plan is to decrease substantially the numbers of handicapped people resident in hospitals, and eventually to close many hospitals altogether.

What do parents know about the various forms of care that are available? There are some parents who have only vaguely heard about any residential provision, their son or daughter never having stayed away from home. Their level of knowledge is often very hazy, arising primarily by word of mouth. There are many parents, in contrast, whose son or daughter has spent short periods of time in a local hostel. Finally, there are a few parents whose son or daughter has had experience of living away for a much longer period, sometimes a few months, sometimes many years. The son or daughter, for a variety of reasons, has come back to live at home, often with an expectation that he or she will remain there for the forseeable future.

Differences of view

From these varying bases of knowledge and experience, parents have very mixed views about the available forms of care. Some have nothing but praise for the care arrangement their son or daughter has experienced; some have a more cautious view, noting some good and bad features; and some are highly critical – even appalled – by what they have seen. These differing views arise in part from the varying qualities of different arrangements, in part from parents' individual preferences and in part from the differing needs of their sons and daughters. What pleases one parent may horrify another simply because of the individual needs of the handicapped person concerned.

Not surprisingly, what parents say they like and dislike about the arrangements experienced mirror what they advocate or seek to avoid, as explored above. For instance, the features that please parents are 'personal attention', 'being well looked after', 'nice, caring staff', 'good company', 'having lots of things to do', 'having their own room', a 'bright and clean environment', and most important of all, a 'homely atmosphere'. Conversely, the aspects that displease parents are 'lack of care', 'inadequate supervision', 'too many residents', insufficient attention to 'safety', an 'institutional atmosphere' and so on.

These experiences can be best brought to life by giving the account of three families. All have direct experience of hostel provision, in two cases for short-term care and in one case for the long term.

First, there is the experience of David, aged 42, living with his parents who are in their seventies. He has a mild mental handicap but also some physical disabilities and he has to use a wheelchair when going any distance. He recently spent two short spells in a local hostel, at the suggestion of a social worker, apparently conscious of his parents' age. The hostel had 16 residents, grouped into four sections of four; residents were expected to do what they could for themselves, although some help was provided with cooking.

According to his parents, David very much enjoyed the time he spent there: 'He didn't want to come home, he said he'd like to stay'. To some extent, his parents likened the experience to a holiday:

> You don't like a holiday to finish do you?... I could understand his feelings, though, because you see all the young people there, records and that. He loves records and discos and although he can't take part in dancing, they do try and make him get up.

David's parents view the hostel with some concern:

> Well if I'm honest, I don't think the staff is really up to standard. There doesn't seem anybody around. Now, I took his hold-all down with his overnight changes and that and I don't think he had a change in four days, did he? [His clothes] were in the bag just the same as when he left home. He said he had a bath in the middle of the week but why not put clean clothes on? [Perhaps] they left it to David to sort of choose his clothes, because I always do that for him.
>
> We did look over it, when it was brand new. Well, it looked nice, spotlessly clean. But obviously if you get 16 boys or girls running round on carpets, beds unmade, things are going to get spilled. . . . I don't think they clean the place up quite like you do your own home. Well, I don't think they get enough time. . . . And another thing I didn't like, one of the boys who was working with David all day had to go back to prepare tea for them. I didn't think that was a very good idea. Well, I should have thought that there'd be someone there to prepare a meal.

Secondly, there is the experience of Paul, in his early thirties, who has Down's Syndrome. His parents, who are in their early seventies, say he is a happy and very active person: 'He always likes having something to do.' He has spent a week or two in two different hostels. Again, Paul seemed to enjoy his time away, but his parents felt both hostels were far from ideal:

> They tend to stick them in a lounge, put them in front of a television set; it's not home – family home-wise. It's not homely, it's big and it's a problem because they have all sorts of capacities and different types. There's a lot of young part-timers that run them, which to me is not right, really you want a mother or father figure. They're young, rather offhandish, although it may be a good idea that they are all known by their Christian names, but it needs to be more stable. . . .
>
> The other hostel was very badly conceived in so far as it is in the same complex, or within a stone's throw of the occupational centre, so they don't even get the stimulation of going out from the place where they live. It's rather unimaginative to go out to work and just walk across the yard. See, they're committing this crime in my estimation.

Finally, there is Matthew. He is 24 and also has Down's Syndrome. He has now left home and gone to live in a local hostel. He went there because his mother, in her sixties, was concerned that he should be settled before anything happened to her. When a 24-place hostel was opened in the area, she took the place. Here are her comments, after two years:

> I was very disappointed in some respects. When Matthew went in, they took them in groups of eight which was ideal, but they now have all different types – people with behaviour problems, disturbed girls who would scream every meal time. I feel very strongly about this: this is going to be their home for life and it's imperative when they go to their hostel at nights there should be some modicum of serenity, more like home life. . . . When this hostel was on the drawing board, they thought of 20–24, they've changed since, they want smaller units and I'm all for them. I'd say eight is quite enough. They are short staffed and they have admitted that they are short staffed. Because they didn't envisage people coming in having fits. They've had the incontinent, they have three or four in wheelchairs, it wasn't built for that. . . . The staff I can't speak highly enough of. They are lovely. They are totally dedicated, they are

hard-working, they are kind, they are caring. This is very important that they are caring. But with all the good will in the world, if they don't have enough staff, then that's just going to fall through.

Although Matthew's mother thinks the hostel is ill-conceived in form and short-staffed for the needs of the residents, she is delighted with the way in which her son has developed since he went to live there:

> Oh, he goes out, they go to the pub sometimes and he goes to club and they have meetings and they are consulted. And when Matthew asked for a meeting, I couldn't believe it, that my child, my son, was saying, 'meeting, please'. . . . Matthew is more rounded now, I think that's the description; he is a more rounded person, he is a personality now. Matthew is a person now. He wasn't, he was my little boy here.

These parents all note some good and some bad points with regard to the hostels experienced. They also, however, have different expectations of what is good for their sons. David's parents, for instance, do not like the fact that his hostel is training people to be more independent. His mother, who does everything for him at home, admits that he could do more for himself, but she has a very clear view about 'a mum's role'. Her son is still a child and she would not expect any child of hers to have to make a meal, wash his clothes, even choose his own clothes. Matthew's mother, in contrast, welcomes the strides in independence made by her son through the hostel. All recognize the difficulties of running a hostel, especially in trying to suit everyone: in Paul's father's words: 'How can you have 100 per cent perfect homes for 20 or 30 people who've got different handicaps, different mentalities. . . . It's easy to criticize but how do you lay down a system?'

It is evident, however, that there is a serious mismatch between what parents would like for their son or daughter and what is currently available. While some of their requirements might be subsequently adapted in the light of experience, their arguments deserve attention. Their case is based on a close understanding of what they feel their sons or daughters need. Parents' call for a small, homely living environment is full of reason. Moreover, the gap between what is wanted and what exists clearly slows up the process of letting go.

CHAPTER 6

Planning and Undergoing a Move

Your family, everything's in stages, isn't it. You get married, you have your children, they grow up and go. But, you see, the pattern doesn't happen here. One doesn't go.... So now we're saying, 'he's 29, now he must have a life for himself'. It's something we can't provide. It's something he can't provide on his own. So he's going to need help from the Social Services. Now it's trying to find the right thing for him.

Mother of Arthur, aged 29

The complexity of parents' views on making the break, their efforts to develop more general independence and their views of alternative provision have all now been explored. But what is it really like to see a son or daughter leave home? What preparations are especially crucial? How do parents feel after the event? This chapter is devoted to these questions.

Thinking about a move

There are two clear steps which need to be taken in planning for a son or daughter to leave home. The first is taking the decision that this is the desirable course; the second is the making and effecting of a particular plan. But what makes parents decide that the time has come?

For many parents, the need to think about a move arises as they find themselves getting on in years. They realize that some provision needs to be made before they can no longer cope and want to play an active part in the decision process. They want to see their son or daughter 'settled' and to know what the care will be like. As one mother says: 'I wanted her to go somewhere where, if she wasn't happy or if I wasn't happy with it, I could have her home and then start again from square one.' Sometimes an additional spur is given by the death of one partner or a friend of a similar age. This serves to remind parents of their own mortality.

Some parents are particularly concerned about the needs of other members of their family, especially other children who may have lost out in terms of attention: 'I think it's right for everybody else [in the family]. You must have heard it said quite a few times, it's not a handicapped child, it's a handicapped family.' Others simply want some time to themselves. This is, after all, normally the case for parents of non-handicapped children. They want to be able to pursue their own interests and to have the ability to come and go as they like. As one mother explains:

> It's only recently, as the other children get older, you expect a bit of freedom like everyone else. And it's only then that you begin to think that you may never get it. Because your other friends are free to go out and your teenage children can look after themselves, but you're different as a family.

A few parents also feel that an early move is in the interest of their son or daughter. In some families, this may be because he or she is felt to be bored or lonely at home. In others, it is more a matter of ensuring that the move is undertaken at a point when the son or daughter is feeling secure, not when it is a time of great crisis. Occasionally, also, handicapped sons and daughters initiate the subject of a move from home. Through friends at their day centre or elsewhere, they become aware of the existence of other places to live, such as local hostels. It is not surprising that some wish to sample life elsewhere. Indeed, a few are aware of the precariousness of their own position in the home of ageing parents and are concerned to ensure that they have somewhere to go.

Some parents simply come to a point of exhaustion from looking after their son or daughter. They can become quite desperate. One father of a severely epileptic son, given to violence, notes:

> We've more or less gone into everything. I don't think we've missed anybody out. I even thought of trying to more or less

bribe someone to get him in somewhere, a good place, you know. Make them an offer of so much money to try to get somewhere permanent for him.

Someone to talk to

There is no question that a concerned outsider can play an important part in addressing this issue. In some cases this central role is played by another son or daughter. Mothers find themselves being nagged to look into alternative care by a concerned sibling, perhaps recognizing the need for some intervention in this way. Sometimes these siblings are themselves concerned about what will be expected of them in the long term. Professional involvement on this question – from a social worker, doctor or staff at the training centre – can also prove useful. Having someone to talk to not only provides an additional source of information but also acts as a stimulus for pursuing the issue. Furthermore, and of great importance, it enables parents to share the burden of the decision.

The significance of this catalyst role is commonly highlighted by its absence; a number of parents speak of their wish for someone to take the step of raising the issue with them. One mother puts this in terms of giving parents an early reminder about the issue: 'Social workers could . . . approach it and say, "have you got any plans for when so and so gets older?" It might sow a seed that they will begin to think along these lines.' Some involvement of this kind also helps to reduce their own responsibility for taking 'the terrible decision'. As one mother states with respect to the social workers: 'If they would say to me, "now, look, you're being unkind to your daughter, it's time she was on her own", then I would say straight away, "well, if you really think that, that I'm doing her more harm than good, then I would have no say in the matter".' This is particularly crucial for those parents who feel they are likely to be criticized for 'putting her away'. As the same mother continues: 'I don't want them to think I am pushing my child on. I want them to . . . come forward and say, "we would like to have her". Then I should be happy.'

Where such a move is desired, of course, there is not always available provision. Some families are actively concerned to find a place for their son or daughter, but have no idea of where he or she can go. In a few families, this is simply a lack of information; they have not really learned about the local hostel or other arrangements for care. More commonly, however, it appears to be a lack of any suitable place. Particularly among those parents whose son's or daughter's handicap is very severe, there is a real problem of finding anywhere appropriate. Indeed, one impetus for a move can be the opening up of a new home for handicapped people, especially if parents feel there is unlikely to be another one for some time. Again, parents of sons and daughters with a severe handicap may be particularly eager to accept a place, if the only alternative is the local hospital, since the opportunity may not arise again for several years.

Preparations towards a move

The development of full independence of a son or daughter takes a very long time. This is true for non-handicapped children as well as handicapped ones. Over the years, parents try to teach what they see as the necessary skills and impart what they see as the necessary attitudes. When the time is right, they often try out occasional separations from their son or daughter. In ordinary households, the children quickly learn that they are working towards the development of full independence, leaving the parental home to set up on their own. Many, of course, cannot wait to go. But what happens where this independence is likely to be restricted because of a handicap?

Parents of handicapped sons and daughters who have made this break stress the importance of the preparations towards it. The slow development of independence, both the ability to carry out the ordinary tasks of everyday life and the lessening of emotional dependence on parents, is central here. The use of short-term care, often over a period of years, is also crucial in helping both parents and their son or daughter to become accustomed to separation – 'a sort of leading-up over the years'. Both of these have been explored in Chapter 4. But there is also the need to discuss the issue with their son or daughter, to create some understanding of what it is all about.

Talking it over

Parents seem to find it very difficult to talk about the question of leaving home with their mentally handicapped son or daughter. It is a sensitive and emotive subject and one which can rarely be broached in any kind of easy or objective way. Parents often say that they feel he or she would never understand, in some cases because the handicap is too severe, but in others because the issue is so hard to grasp. There is also a dilemma if there is no obvious problem: 'If I was feeling ill, perhaps then she would grasp what the meaning was . . .'

With non-handicapped children, the issue of leaving home is usually raised by the son or daughter, rather than the parent. They take the initiative to move away, often as part of the developing of independence which arises in a person's late teens or early twenties: 'They make up their own minds' one mother notes, whereas in the case of her handicapped daughter, 'you don't know if she wants to go, if she's frightened to leave us or not'.

One reason for not raising the issue is parents' belief that their son or daughter would not want to leave home. Much of this is based on actual experience of life elsewhere. As has been shown, many handicapped people have stayed in a local hostel on a temporary basis and therefore have some idea of what it is like. Parents often say that their sons and daughters enjoy such visits, but do not want to live there on a long-term basis: 'I've spoken to her about the hostel several times. She'll say, "I don't mind a weekend, Mummy, I don't mind a week. But I wouldn't like to live there." ' Another mother similarly notes: 'Now, I think our Dorothy would like to live in a hostel. She talks about it, but only if something happened to me or her dad. She says, "while ever I've got this home, I'm happy here". And, well, she is.'

The problem is intensified in those families where moving to the hostel has been posed as an occasional threat to the handicapped person. All families have arguments and in their anger may talk about means of getting away from one another. Families with handicapped children are no exception; indeed, because of the stresses, the arguments may be more frequent. Handicapped sons and daughters occasionally threaten to run away from home – even try to do it – when angry with their parents. On the other side, some parents admit with some guilt that they have occasionally threatened to send their son or daughter to the local hostel: 'When he's been getting awkward here, and he can you know, I've said, "they ought to put thee in that bloody hostel and they'd know how carry-on tha's got". . . . I've threatened him with that, haven't I?'

But as the time arises, some parents take great pains to explain to their son or daughter the need to move from home. Those with other children find it easier to make comparisons with them and the fact that they are living elsewhere. One mother, trying to ease her son's transition from home, explains:

> The way I approached it was to say 'You're the eldest. One sister's gone, the other's going. [They've] got their own friends, living their own life now.... I left my mum and dad. There comes a time when this happens. This is what everybody does.'

The process of preparing for the move is a long one. It is not something which any family feels can be accomplished at all quickly. Whatever the processes undertaken, whatever the elaborate preparations made, there is a strong feeling among parents that 'you're never ready'. The break is simply too big an event to ever be fully prepared for it. Those who have been through it suggest that there is a tendency to go through the motions of preparation with an air of unreality. Indeed, they often comfort themselves with the hope that the day will not come; as one mother says: 'I hoped that [the hostel] would say, "we can't accept him, he won't fit in", or "we've got too many on the waiting list".'

Just before the move

The period immediately preceding the move is a particularly upsetting one, as it is a time in which the decision can be reviewed and, in principle, reversed. The desire to go back on the decision can be very strong: 'I think you feel guilty that you are throwing them into the outside world.' There is a tendency to look out for disapproval from others around them and, possibly, use this as an excuse to change course: 'I think if my other children had said to me, "you are being wicked, you are sending her away", then she wouldn't have gone.' Where the waiting period is extended unexpectedly, parents find it particularly difficult. In contrast, when the move is effected quickly, parents feel themselves to be fortunate. There is a sense of being 'dazed' during this period, reeling with a confused mixture of apprehension and relief: 'You had to keep saying to yourself, it's for Catherine: it's better for her, it's better for her.'

This is also a period when the question of preparing for a move becomes all too real. It is a time when hostel staff may visit the home to help get to know the son or daughter in a comfortable surrounding. Equally, it is a time of regular visits of the son or daughter to the hostel to become familiar with the other residents and the routine there. Parents try to make the whole thing sound exciting and something to look forward to: 'I used to say, "lovely room" when we used to talk about it. I used to say, "lovely room, James, won't it be lovely?" and he would say, "yes", oh, bless his heart.'

The period before a move is also a difficult one for the handicapped son or daughter. Some may not understand what is going on and some parents say they find this easier. At least there is no sense that they are forcing something he or she does not want to do. Others, however, have some understanding: 'He didn't say much. I think he was quite excited, what he would do. It was going to be something new, something different. When we went to the hostel, he very much sat there and looked at the others.' Where there have been a number of short stays at the same hostel, the transition may be greatly eased.

Seeing them go

The experience of parting from a son or daughter can be a deeply distressing one. There is a feeling of sheer sadness at separation, combined in some cases with a feeling of betrayal: 'Other children go of their own choice. I'm sending her, you know.'

Parents' own needs can be very strong here. There is a recognition of the need to 'come to terms' with the situation: 'See yourself warts and all, see yourself being a bit selfish and being sorry for yourself.' In addition, there is the sense of seeing the end of a particular way of life. Here is one mother in her sixties:

> Well, it's so final, isn't it. This is the thing, it is the finality of it all ... I knew that once he went, that was it. That he would be there, that's that, for the rest of his life and the rest of my natural life. So therefore it was a very difficult thing to do.

Moving day can be particularly traumatic: 'It was awful; it was really awful. ... I remember it so well, that day. I couldn't stay there ... I more or less took my son in and when he started unpacking his case, I just came out. I just didn't want to stay there.'

Another puts it this way: 'I just wanted to cry, but I couldn't. I couldn't let Joseph see me unhappy, this was it. So there was all this bottled up.' Some parents note they were greatly helped by family or friends taking them out afterwards to distract them, but few find it other than a very difficult event. Elderly mothers who have to return to an empty house, with the knowledge that there is no one to cook for and look after, feel this, perhaps, most strongly.

Some parents liken the period immediately after the move to a period of bereavement. This is partly in their own sense of loss: 'It was myself I was sorry for. It's like grief in death, you weep for yourself, you weep for your loneliness.' Perhaps more distressing, this is also seen in other people's reactions: 'People don't ask you about it; they don't like to approach the subject because of upsetting you.' The problem is compounded where parents are asked to give their son or daughter a period in which to settle down and therefore do not see him or her: 'If you can't cope, your immediate reaction is to go down there and get them.' This period can be made significantly easier, however, where hostels are approachable and sympathetic to this problem. A policy of enabling parents to phone frequently to discuss their son or daughter can be particularly useful.

There is no doubt that, particularly for women who have been caring for a handicapped son or daughter on their own, the loss of the company and involvement is overwhelming. There is an inevitable change in the daily routine. As one mother explains: 'It's seeing the coaches at nights at first, you know, go past. It goes up the road here, and, oh, wishing he was coming home.' And another, 'It is a bit heart rending, you know, to go past her room and it's just as you left it.' Most difficult of all is the terrible feeling of loss of someone loved: 'I only realized it later. I could see that I needed my son more than he needed me. If you're honest about it, you do as you get older. You need someone. I'm a touching person, so I missed this very vital thing for me, the touch.'

Starting to adjust

Once the initial period is over, however, parents tend to find that they begin to cope and, to their own surprise, to relax. This takes a considerable period of time. It is particularly difficult to adjust to the enormous freedom they gain, just to come and go as they liked; one mother explains: 'It takes you a long time to realize that your life is your own now; to a certain extent it's yours. . . . It takes a long time to get used to that freedom.' And another: 'It took some adjusting. I had to stop myself looking at the clock every afternoon because she would normally be coming back.'

The transition is eased where parents are able to keep in frequent touch with their son or daughter. A common scenario is a weekly visit by parents to the hostel and trips home for the weekend once a month or so. This helps parents to feel that their son or daughter is not 'put away' and that relations are maintained in much the same way as with married children: 'The joy of it is that she is so close to me, so that if she is ill, they could ring up and one could be there in minutes.'

Furthermore, from their son's and daughter's point of view, many parents find themselves delighted with the extent to which there is a change: 'Looking back on it, she led a pretty lonely life. . . . It was just the two of us, you know. I think she needed the stimulation of other people's company.' Many find their son or daughter develops a new independence, not readily fostered at home: 'She's much quicker mentally, much quicker responses to things; her vocabulary has improved and she tackles all sorts of jobs.' Here is another mother talking:

> We protect them to such an extent that we think they are incapable. I mean, we arrange their holiday, we arrange this and tell them what to do. I mean, we pick out the clothes they are going to wear. Whereas now she makes her own choice . . . I thought I had got her to do as much as she was capable of doing. But I have learned since that I hadn't.

Parents are also helped where they see that their son or daughter really has a new 'home'. One mother says: 'She's got her own life now', and another, *'he's* let go of *me'*. The sense of a separate home is a development few parents seem to have expected, but is gives them enormous pride. One mother comments:

> And I feel I'm in Luke's home and they make me feel that. . . . I feel I am going into my son's home. I never knocked on Luke's bedroom door. They are giving him dignity. You know, this is lovely. Even I didn't give him that dignity. Well, he was only my little boy, wasn't he?

One father, speaking of his daughter Mary's weekend visit home, notes that on returning to the hostel, having thanked him for a lovely time, 'she turns to me and says, "I'm going to my room now, Dad" ... and she's away. She's quite happy and that's great. That's all I need.'

The separation between parent and child can be difficult in any family. Parents are commonly apprehensive about the changes about to be experienced by a son or daughter leaving home, while knowing that their own lives must carry on in a new way. But where the son or daughter has a mental handicap, there is a very great poignancy in seeing him or her settled. As one mother puts it simply: 'The relief of knowing that if anything happens to me, he is all right. And that is worth all the grief, all the tears, all the sadness.'

CHAPTER 7

Letting Go: Dilemmas and Responses

> There is the emotional side of you which loves your child
> dearly and you don't want to part with him. There is the
> other side, common sense, which says now is the time, if you
> love him let him go, you are doing it for him. But there is a
> selfish side too, can I manage on my own? I am going to be so
> lonely.
>
> Mother of Martin, aged 24

This book has not sought to make recommendations for individual
families about when a mentally handicapped person should leave
home. It would be inappropriate for anyone outside of a family to
judge for parents where their son or daughter should live or when
a move should take place. Nevertheless, it is clear that there is a
very real problem for parents arising from the fact that in most
families something eventually *has* to be done. If unplanned moves
at a time of crisis or illness are to be avoided, then parents need to
give some advance thought to the possibility of a move. Indeed,
most families are highly concerned about this problem and many
would like help in making what can be one of the most difficult
decisions of their lives.

For parents, there are essentially three questions which need to
be considered. First, there is the need to decide when is the right
time for a son or daughter to leave home. Second, there is the
decision about where their son or daughter will go. Third, there is
the need to prepare for the move from home, to help it take place
as smoothly as possible. In this final chapter, some ways in which
parents may resolve these issues are explored.

Finding the right time to part

It is evident that many parents whose son or daughter has moved from home are delighted and relieved that the break has been made. Whatever the pain it had caused them, they are comforted by the knowledge that if something happens to them, their son or daughter will be all right. Some also experience other positive reactions to the move: a new-found sense of freedom to be themselves and a delight that their son or daughter had more potential to develop than was previously recognized. But parents may need considerable help to reach this point. Social workers, staff at training centres and hostel staff may all help in some way. Support could also be given by other parents, through parent groups. People often find that others 'in the same boat' – more than anyone else – really know what the problems are and can provide the necessary understanding.

Raising the issue

Much of the help which parents need is a matter of having someone to talk to. Ideally, discussion should begin very early, long before a move is to take place. This gives parents time to think about it and get used to the idea well before it is an urgent issue. In addition, it makes it less of an 'unknown' when the time does come. Parents do not find it easy to raise the subject and are often afraid of disapproval, from friends and professionals alike, for 'putting him away'. One mother explains this need with some clarity:

> A lot more counselling is needed, I think, from quite an early age. One would like to be able to go through it stage by stage. If you could sort of talk to people that have that skill. If you could say, 'well, he's 11 now, is he happy where he is? Are you happy where he is? Is there something else?' You know, so that it's a gradual thing. . . . Even if it's only once a year. Just to see that you're not climbing up the wall. Or going to pieces or something . . . . There should be someone that perhaps can make you open up and say, 'well, we have got a bit of a problem.'

Having someone to talk to might involve one of a number of different professionals: a social worker, care worker, day centre staff member or general practitioner or, indeed, someone else. It is not so important *who* helps in this way, as long as there is someone who does. The person who takes on this counselling role must have a good understanding of the conflicting feelings that parents will undoubtedly be experiencing. They will also need to appreciate that the discussions may go on over some time, certainly months and possibly years.

Alternatively, or preferably additionally, another parent might be helpful here, especially one who has already been through the experience of seeing a son or daughter leave home. This can provide a valuable model for parents, and offers opportunities to explore all the details of importance to parents themselves. This suggestion was itself put by one parent whose son had left home after great doubts on her part: 'I'd love to go to some of the parents and let them see how happy I am now.' This was almost entirely due to the benefits she saw for her son, but it was also due to her own relief that a suitable arrangement had been made for him.

These discussions, either on a group or a one-to-one basis, could be organized through a local parents' organization, such as the local Mencap Society, a parents' association centred on a day centre or even an informal parents group within a neighbourhood. Again, what is important is not where they take place but that some opportunities are offered for them to take place at all. Parents do not easily open up their inner thoughts on this issue, however, even with other parents. There may be a need for someone, such as one parent willing to talk about his or her own feelings, to get the discussion underway.

Need for information

Parents also have a need for much fuller information about the kinds of residential provision available to them. They need opportunities to learn about what there is, how many people live there, what the staff are like and so forth. There are a mass of both major and minor questions for which parents need answers. Some may seem trivial, but are crucial to parents' confidence in alternative care arrangements. Essentially, they need to know what life would be like for their son or daughter if a move from home were to take place.

It should not be difficult for authorities to put together a package of information for parents of handicapped people. This could include information on a wide variety of needs and services, including alternative care arrangements. The latter should cover information on local hotels and other residential provision, the authority's policy on sponsoring places outside the area and other sources of help. It should also call attention to ways in which parents can be assisted to think about – and prepare for – the move from home. At the very least, a file in local libraries with this information should be available and widely publicized.

Parents also need the kind of information that can only come from talking to people who provide residential provision. They need to feel that they can visit local places to see what they are about. There is an inevitable conflict in not trespassing on the privacy of residents, but visits during the day should not be a problem. Staff should try to think about the kinds of questions to which parents – and their son or daughter – will want answers. They should encourage them to make more than one visit. What is important is making the place seem open and accessible, a place families feel they know and can come to know even better.

Developing independence and undergoing preparations

But once the issue has been raised and parents informed about the choices open to them, the time may still not seem right for a move. There are a number of points on which parents will first need to feel satisfied. One is that their son or daughter has developed a sufficient feeling of independence to cope on his or her own. This is partly a question of having the appropriate practical skills and partly one of emotional independence from the parents.

Parents may need some help and advice, often over many years, about the development of their son's or daughter's independence. This tends to be a very sensitive issue, as no one likes to be told how to bring up his or her child. Furthermore, parents are understandably reluctant to let their handicapped son or daughter take risks. Some parents find that others outside the home are more able to teach their son or daughter than they are, not because they are not good teachers, but because – as with non-handicapped children – the close relationship between parent and child can make teaching difficult.

One means of encouraging independence, and preparing the

way towards a move, is the use of short breaks for the son or daughter, first occasionally and then on a regular basis. There is a need for readily available short-term ('respite') care of an acceptable standard for this purpose. Respite care is commonly advocated both to ensure a source of help in emergencies and to provide parents with an occasional break from their caring responsibilities. But short stays outside the home play a key role in the process of helping parents and their son or daughter to learn to live independently of each other. They provide an excellent opportunity to experience a period of separation on a trial basis.

For mentally handicapped people, a short stay away from the parental home allows them to establish themselves outside of the 'child' role and to see other ways of living at first hand. They can begin to get a taste of having their own territory and their own friends outside the home; this may help them to decide whether their parents' home is the most appropriate place to be. At the same time, a short break can be very important for parents. They may find that they are not indispensable and their son or daughter can survive – even enjoy life – away from their care. While both parents and offspring may miss each other, the experience of separation can help to loosen the ties of dependency. Indeed, contrary to conventional expectations, it may make parents more – rather than less – willing to let their son or daughter leave home.

Some families take up an offer of short-term care with some enthusiasm. Others, however, find it difficult to accept, even for one night away. Among these are likely to be those families who are putting off the issue of a move from home. If short-term care is to be useful to such families, there will be a need for some encouragement to use it. The positive aspects of a stay for their son or daughter should be pointed out, particularly for a sense of confidence in the long-run. This may make it much easier for parents to explore this option.

Where will they go?

There is no point in parents beginning to think through a move of their son or daughter from home unless there is somewhere for him or her to go. Furthermore, this must be somewhere that parents consider suitable, if not their preferred arrangement. Parents have strong views on what any future home for their son or daughter should be like and their views should be taken seriously. This is partly because they have a close understanding of the kind of environment their son or daughter needs. But it is also because they will inevitably play a large part in the choice of any future home. Indeed, their view about the right time to part will inevitably be affected by where they think he or she would go to live.

Parents do not have a uniform view about residential care; they seek a range of kinds of provision. This is due partly to different individual preferences and partly to the very differing needs of their sons and daughters. But it is striking that parents seek one common feature. Whatever the kind of housing, whatever the size and location, the place should feel like 'home' to the people who live there.

The need for more 'homes'

The need for more provision, given the numbers of ageing parents with sons and daughters at home, needs no underlining; it does not need to be argued here. But several comments might be added about parents' views. First, they are not largely in conflict with current professional thinking about the needs of people with a mental handicap. Their desire for a small, homely, caring, secure and permanent environment would receive strong support, at least in principle, from a host of people working in this field. For some years, many have been calling for smaller living units based in ordinary housing. Similarly, parents' dislike of hospitals and other large institutions is very much in line with current policy.

Second, whatever their hopes, parents seem very ready to compromise. In practice, many accept what they see to be reasonable and do not hold out for the ideal. They accept provision which is far from the desired small home with a 'family' atmosphere. Many parents believe that their son or daughter will eventually go to live in a hostel, whatever their reservations about this form of care. It is difficult to see what choice they have. There is only a limited amount of accommodation available, places in more imaginative forms of care are scarce and private homes are beyond the means of most families. Parents have thus had to accept that what they would wish for their handicapped child is by no means the same as what they are likely to get.

The lack of alternatives for people with a severe handicap

Some attention must be drawn to parents who have sons or daughters with a severe handicap. In general, it is these parents who have the most serious reservations about the forms of care that are currently available. Yet they are the ones who are in most need of a suitable alternative arrangement. Under greatest stress in their day-to-day lives, they need alternative care to give them a break as well as somewhere for the longer term. When they look around them, however, all they normally see are large hospitals which are being run down, minimally-staffed hostels with great emphasis on training for independence, and group homes which cater exclusively for those with milder handicaps. It is not surprising that some of these parents are very angry:

> One of the most awful things is the lack of understanding on the part of the authorities. . . . They think it's doing us a tremendous favour giving us the odd break here and there. . . . They totally lack imagination and they totally lack a will to help. Money is spent on all [kinds of] other things that we regard as far less important than actually looking after the least advantaged people in the community . . . and here we are struggling like mad to survive, you know, sort of practically drowning and nobody cares a damn.

Parents have very clear views about what makes for good residential care arrangements. They also need to feel trust in what is provided in order to contemplate any move from home. Their participation in planning and organizing care provision should be sought as one means of ensuring that their views are heard. While some seek to set up their own arrangements, for instance through parent organizations, this is unlikely to add more than a small proportion of the provision needed. There is also a real question about the extent to which parents who have cared for a son or daughter over many years should feel they have to spend their 'spare' time running voluntary schemes.

Making the move go smoothly

Moves are unsettling for anyone. Most people like to feel at home in their surroundings and establish a certain routine. Moves mean a change in these important aspects of ordinary living. In the circumstances under discussion here, they entail a change in who people live with, who they see each morning, who they discuss the details of the day with each night. This is the case not only for the handicapped son or daughter but also for the parent or parents left behind in their home. Undergoing a move is clearly difficult for all involved; the separation necessarily brings with it the establishment of a new and different life.

Parents are likely to need considerable help during the period of transition. They need to be able to talk about the changes to be experienced and their feelings about them. They need to come to accept that some sadness is natural in the circumstances, but that there is likely to be a positive side. They also need to be assured that while the parting may mean a change in where their son or daughter lives, there should be no change in their fondness for one another. Parents do not 'lose' their son or daughter through a move, just as they do not do so when a non-handicapped child leaves home. Indeed, they can continue to see each other both through weekend visits to the parents' home by the son or daughter and through visits by the parents to his or her new home. Parents may also need to be assured that, although not a desirable outcome, the decision can be reversed if the arrangement is unsuccessful. All of these assurances would make the transitional period much easier.

At the same time, the handicapped son or daughter will also need someone to talk to about the move. The perspective here is likely to be different. He or she may not have made the choice to move and may be less able to anticipate the implications of any change. There will again be a need for reassurance that both love and contact will continue with the parents left behind. Different people may need to be involved here, with special skills or knowledge of the handicapped person. Family and friends may be particularly helpful; so, too, may those who have a relationship through the daily routine, such as staff at day centres.

Seeing a son or daughter leave home is not simply a question of finding a place for him or her to live. A key issue is the nature of the support which will be available, either from professional sources, such as a social worker or residential staff, or simply family and friends. Parents quite rightly worry about who will visit their son or daughter and generally act in the role of a close friend. Of course, they can do so themselves for some time, but there is also concern about the long-term future when they are no longer there to do so. Those with other children commonly express the hope that they will keep an eye on their brother or sister in this way.

Moves from home are not likely to happen without a lot of pain and worry. Few mentally handicapped people or their parents experience no qualms. But with proper planning, successful moves do occur, leaving everyone feeling settled and happy. Here is one mother's description of how she feels a move should be:

> Probably [the move] would be a gradual sort of thing, hoping that he would be so happy that you'd go one day and he'd say, 'no, I don't want to come home with you. I want to stay here because it's more fun'. That's the ideal thing, that he would say, 'no, it's more fun here. I've got my friends here. I don't want to come home'.

How things can go wrong

It cannot be said, of course, that every move of a handicapped person is permanent or successful. There are places which parents find unacceptable, there are sons and daughters who refuse to stay and there are arrangements which break down for some other reason. One of the side effects of such problems is that both the mentally handicapped person and the parents have to readjust to living together again. This, in itself, can be difficult. But in addition, the separation process has to be gone through all over again. A brief comment must be added here about these 'failed moves', if only to alert others to the potential difficulties which may arise.

The current policy of running down mental handicap hospitals means that there are some parents who find their son or daughter back living with them. Although it is the normal policy to arrange alternative residential care, not all parents are willing to accept this and take the option of bringing their son or daughter back home. This is a difficult situation for all concerned and parents may need opportunities to explore the likely changes in some detail. Hospital staff should ensure that sufficient time is devoted to parents' concerns.

There are also some parents who feel that their son or daughter is so unhappy in alternative care that they bring him or her home to live. The reasons for not settling, of course, are various. Some simply miss the life they led at home: 'He misses us terribly . . . it's his room, and his belongings, his possessions.' Others find it difficult to manage for one reason or another, for instance with a wheelchair in an environment not suited to it. Such experiences can have a considerable effect: 'Now he doesn't want to go away unless he's got to go. This is his home.'

It is not always the parents who decide to bring their son or daughter home. Sometimes, it is a social worker or other professional who suggests that a return home might be best. But there are also some mentally handicapped people who refuse to stay away. They simply walk out and find their way home. Parents can find this particularly trying; here is one father, whose thirty-four-year-old son insists he wants to live at home:

> He's got this fairy tale world that things are never going to change. . . . On occasion, when his mother and I have said to him, 'look, if this goes on, your mum and I are pulling out, we're leaving this house and going', [he replies] 'Oh, well, that's all right, whoever comes in will let me have my room.'

In some families, there is a long history of moves back and forth. The last move home may prove as gradual as the move away can be. Visits home become more frequent and longer:

> He didn't want to go back, both he and I were finding it very traumatic, I didn't like leaving him and he didn't like going and then one day . . . we just decided we weren't going to take him back anymore and see how we would cope.

There are also families who, having placed their son or daughter in residential care for some years, decide to bring him or her home for 'a taste of home life'. This can work well, although considerable adjustments, not always foreseen, need to be made. But it can also prove a real problem. Undertaken with the most selfless of motives, such arrangements can go disastrously wrong. Both the parents and the son or daughter can find it difficult to adjust to the new circumstances:

> For the first few weeks, it was a novelty to him, it was a novelty to us and everything was lovely. . . . And then things gradually – well, you're tied down, there's nothing you can do, you can't go out together. . . . He gradually got into the rut of just coming home, having his tea upstairs, sitting on his bed . . . and we don't see him no more.

A son or daughter may also change on his or her return to home, not always for the better. This may be because adapting to what is essentially a new life can be difficult for a handicapped person. But it is also easy for strides in independence, made when living elsewhere, to begin to slip, especially where parents do not want to be strict. Inertia, coupled with parents' own possibly slow routine, may mean that fewer efforts are made to help the son or daughter get out and do things: 'Since we've had him home, he's withdrawn and he's just happy on his own. When he was over at the hospital, he was out and enjoying himself all the time.'

These difficulties call attention to the need for particular care when mentally handicapped people are being moved. The tendency to make some decision about where a handicapped person will live, with little consultation or prior discussion with ⁺he person most concerned, means that an already difficult situation is made worse than may be necessary. Moves are invariably stressful when they are from the place viewed as home over many years. Few non-handicapped people would cope easily if such important changes in their circumstances were imposed on them in the same way. While not all moves, however well planned, will prove successful, there is a need for careful thought to the needs of those most deeply affected.

Involving the whole family

This discussion has been concerned with helping parents to begin thinking about the move of their son or daughter from home. But it is equally important for these issues to be explored with mentally handicapped people themselves. The parents' views described throughout these chapters represent only one part of the story.

The case for giving greater attention to helping people with a mental handicap say what *they* want is self-evident. There is, indeed, considerable interest in finding ways of doing this. The growing number of self-advocacy groups provide one example, wherein people with a handicap come together to talk about issues which concern them and to express their needs to those around them. Another example are various kinds of workers, paid professionals as well as voluntary befrienders, who see their task as helping individuals to voice their own particular views. Increasingly, social and health services professionals are seeing it as essential that the views of the 'consumers' are sought in the planning and delivery of services.

Through these processes, people with a mental handicap may increasingly come to think about the issues involved in undertaking a move from home. They may also begin to initiate, more often than in the past, the process of making the break. Just as many parents need help with this question, so their sons and daughters may need help too. Those who come into regular contact with them – staff in day centres, for instance – should offer their support as someone to talk to about what a break would entail.

Once a mentally handicapped person has left the parental home, there is a real need for continuing emotional support. This is particularly important as one of the basic needs provided at home is a sense of security and the feeling of being cared for. When most people leave home, they do so either to get married or to live directly or indirectly with others who provide them with a great deal of this support. For mentally handicapped people, the great majority of whom are unlikely to marry, it can prove much more difficult. It is not easy to secure close friendships. Yet such support is equally important for their welfare. Greater attention, both before they leave home and after they have moved, needs to be given to this issue.

Another group whose needs should be addressed are siblings, in particular the brothers and sisters who agree to take on the responsibility for a handicapped person when the parents die. This book has not dealt with their problems, but it would appear that there are substantial numbers either currently looking after a brother or sister or expecting to do sometime in the future. Many are undoubtedly happy to be in this situation and coping well, but there will be others who find themselves with little sense of choice and little vocation for the work. The opportunity to discuss their needs, and perhaps to meet with others in a similar situation, is likely to be welcomed.

Some concluding comments

It is not easy to be a parent. Whatever the many joys of bringing up children, there are also considerable difficulties along the way. There are a whole host of restrictions on parents' ability to do what they want, most strongly felt when they become parents for the first time. There are the many demands of growing children for attention and stimulation, as well as the need to provide for their physical and emotional needs. As children become adolescents and develop their own interests, parents have to make decisions about how much independence to give them, how much to enable them to do what they want, rather than what they believe to be best. Throughout this process, many parents find it difficult to be sure that the course they chose was 'right'.

Parents with handicapped children have all these problems writ large. To the outside world, their most visible problem is the stress of coping with the demands and limitations of caring for a child with a handicap. They tend to have both extra work in the home and additional restrictions on their freedom, compared to other parents. The job of teaching their son or daughter, and coping with the risks of everyday life, is also that much more difficult. But once their son or daughter has become adult, most of these parents have become very accustomed to the particular life that they lead. The physical and emotional stresses are not generally the most difficult problem to which they have to respond. As for all parents, the deeper question is whether they are, in the end, doing the best for their child.

Parents of non-handicapped sons and daughters do not have to make so many decisions themselves. As their children grow up and develop their own ideas about what they want to do, parental choice becomes increasingly limited. Parents can try to exert some influence, of course, but they know they will by no means always be successful. At some point, their son or daughter will leave the parental home and will be judged, by parents and child alike, to be independent. The choice of spouse, the choice of job, the choice of where to live and what friends to make are all left to the son or daughter. These matters, for good or ill, are out of parents' hands.

This is clearly not the case for the great majority of parents whose son or daughter has a mental handicap. It is not only that the crucial decision about a move from their home is up to them. Of equal importance are the large number of decisions, made over many years, concerning the development of their son's or daughter's capacity for independence. Parents have had to decide whether to take risks in what is taught within the home, as well as in the freedom given outside it, for instance to find new relationships. There is no clear point at which parents see their sons and daughters as adult, making their own decisions and responsible for themselves. It is these decisions which may have determined whether their son or daughter is able to leave home and what kind of life he or she is able to lead.

Parents whose son or daughter has a mental handicap, then, experience particular dilemmas. They suffer a set of anxieties which other parents never have to face. But, whatever the doubts and difficulties, they can – and should – also experience a very particular pride. Raising their children to adulthood, watching them develop, and then seeing them go – all bring their own particular rewards. Letting go is difficult but it is part of moving on. This is best put in the words of one mother, whose thoughts on the move began this chapter:

> First and foremost, it's your child and it's what happens to them and the benefits they accrue from going away. If you love your child, that is the most important thing to you and that helps you to come to terms with your own loneliness. . . .
> My loneliness has gone . . . because I am happy about my son. That is the reward.

Further Reading

The following books are intended to serve as a guide to those who would like to read further on this subject; they represent by no means a complete bibliography on the subject.

Anderson, David (1982) *Social Work and Mental Handicap*, London, Macmillan.

King's Fund (1980) *An Ordinary Life: comprehensive locally based residential services for mentally handicapped people*, London, King's Fund project paper no 24.

McCormack, Mary (1979) *Away from Home: The mentally handicapped in residential care*, London, Constable.

Mittler, Peter (1979) *People Not Patients*, London, Methuen.

Oswin, Maureen (1984) *They Keep Going Away*, London, King's Fund.

Richardson, Ann and Ritchie, Jane (1986) *Making the Break: Parents' perspectives on adults with a mental handicap leaving the parental home*, London, King's Fund.

Russell, Oliver (1985) *Mental Handicap*, Edinburgh, Churchill Livingstone.

Sanctuary, Gerald (1984) *After I'm Gone: What will happen to my handicapped child?*, London, Souvenir Press.

Shennon, Victoria (1983) *A Home of their Own*, London, Souvenir Press.

Ward, Linda (1982) *People First: Developing services in the community for people with mental handicap*, London, King's Fund project paper no 37.

Wertheimer, Alison (1981) *Living for the Present*, London, Campaign for Mentally Handicapped People.

Whelan, Edward and Speake, Barbara (1979) *Learning to Cope*, London Souvenir Press.

Some Useful Organizations

Advocacy Alliance
115 Golden Lane
London EC1Y 0TJ
(01) 253 2056

CMH (Campaign for People with Mental Handicap)
12A Maddox Street
London W1R 9PL
(01) 491 0727

Contact-a-Family
16 Strutton Ground
London SW1P 2HP
(01) 222 2695

Down's Syndrome Association
12–13 Clapham Common Southside
London SW4 7AA
(01) 720 0008

Independent Development Council for People with Mental Handicap
King's Fund Centre
126 Albert Street
London NW1 7NF
(01) 267 7111

MENCAP
(Royal Society for Mentally Handicapped Children and Adults)
123 Golden Lane
London EC1Y 0RT
(01) 253 9433

MIND
(National Association for Mental Health)
22 Harley Street
London W1N 2ED
(01) 637 0741

National Autistic Society
276 Willesden Lane
London NW2 5RB
(01) 451 3844

National Federation of Gateway Clubs
117 Golden Lane
London EC1Y 0RT
(01) 253 9477

People First
126 Albert Street
London NW1 7NF
(01) 267 6111

Sense: The National Deaf-Blind and Rubella Association
311 Grays Inn Road
London WC1X 8PT
(01) 278 1005

Spastics Society
12 Park Crescent
London W1N 4EQ
(01) 636 5020